THE Teaching Assistant's
HANDBOOK

Peter Gossage · Martin Higgs

pfp

© pfp publishing 2004

pfp is a trading name of Electric Word plc
Reg office: 67-71 Goswell Road
London EC1V 7EP
Registration number: 3934419

Writers Peter Gossage, Martin Higgs

Design PinkFrog

Photography Nicholas James

With special thanks to Oldway Primary School, Paignton, Ilsham C of E
Primary School, Torquay, Collaton St Mary C of E School, Paignton

Printed and bound in the UK.

A catalogue record for this book is available from the British Library.

ISBN 1 904677 05 3

pfp orders and customer services
Freepost Lon20579
London EC1B 1BR
Tel: 020 7251 6569
Fax: 020 7251 9045

www.pfp-publishing.com

CONTENTS

1 YOUR ROLE AND RESPONSIBILITIES

2 WORKING AS A MEMBER OF THE TEAM

3 WORKING WITH THE CHILDREN

Introduction

Your role as a teaching assistant (TA) in a primary school is one that has always been valued by staff, children and school managers. The recent DfES emphasis on developing the role of teaching assistants, and the new roles that have emerged out of the recent changes to teachers' working practices, look set to ensure that your place in school takes on even greater importance.

You may be one of the many TAs who belong to the local community. Your children may have attended the school where you are working and you may have started there as a parent volunteer yourself. As such you can bring a unique perspective to the job, and this can be a very powerful and positive asset to the school.

The potential benefits that teaching assistants offer schools and their children is huge. The DfES and Ofsted have recognised the potential benefits that well-managed, valued and motivated TAs can have to both schools and standards. 'Inspections show that the presence of teaching assistants improves the quality of teaching.' (Ofsted, 2002)

This book is intended to help you in your role in school, looking at all the things you need to know and consider in your life as a TA. From working as a member of the team to preparing 'Plan B', *The Teaching Assistant's Handbook* is an essential part of your toolkit as a TA in today's primary teaching environment.

What's in a name?

The roles and responsibilities of TAs have often evolved on a very school-based, local level. Hence, from LEA to LEA, region to region, or even school to school the job title and job description can vary widely. Few jobs in a school can carry such a wide range of titles to cover a role with such similar responsibilities. The range of titles, including General Assistant (GA), Learning Support Assistant (LSA), Classroom Support Assistant (CSA), Individual Classroom Assistant (ICA) and TA, underlines the need for a nationally agreed language and framework for the work of these valuable support staff.

A definition

The DfES use 'teaching assistant' as their preferred generic term for 'all those in paid employment in support of teachers in primary, special and secondary schools. That includes all those with a general role and others with specific responsibilities for a child, subject area or age group.' (DfES, 2000) This is the term we use throughout this book.

A summary of DfES guidelines

A new role for TAs

The government's changes to the role of TAs in our schools are significant and wide ranging. Individual schools have been leading independent change in TA working practices for a long time. Ofsted have been commenting for many years on how schools utilise TAs, and the DfES have been talking seriously about reform since the late 1990s.

The three key areas within the Government's plans can be summed up as

- a national professional framework and development structure for TAs

- the opportunity to echo, and to build upon, the practice of many successful schools with regard to TAs

- stronger school teams which will benefit all members of the school community.

A new perspective

'Teaching must remodel itself to keep up to date ... Teachers will be spending more of their time on teaching, lesson preparation, assessing individual pupil progress and updating their professional skills supported by a range of other adults employed in schools – teaching assistants, administrative assistants, technical support, instructors and learning mentors – so their time is focused on teaching.

Teaching assistants will be

- supervising classes that are undertaking work set by a teacher, or

- working with small groups of pupils on reading practice

- supervising lunchtime activities and invigilating tests

- giving pastoral and other individual support to pupils, and covering for teacher absence.'

(Estelle Morris – DfES, 2001)

A national agreement

On 15 January 2003, a national agreement was signed between education ministers and key partners, including the local authority employers and school workforce unions, with the exception of the NUT (DfES, 2003). One of the key features of the agreement, which has an impact on the teaching assistant's roles, is

'Contractual changes for teachers to bring about a progressive reduction in teachers' overall hours including the delegation of the following 24 routine non-teaching tasks to "support staff".'

These tasks are listed in the box on the next page.

The agreement was that as of September 2003 teachers would no longer be expected to carry out these tasks on a regular basis. This clearly has an implication for the organisation of TAs and other 'support staff' in our schools. The time needed for them to complete any of these tasks still has to be found and budgeted for.

Reform of support staff roles

The key points of these reforms are an acknowledgement that the contractual changes for teachers will be impossible to deliver without the number and roles of TAs being extended, and the establishment of a new 'high level teaching assistant' role (HLTA).

This has been the subject of debate since the agreement was signed. Central to this debate is the use of HLTAs to take responsibility for the whole class in order to release teachers to undertake other tasks away from the classroom.

'High level teaching assistants will be able to cover classes, and should be able to ensure that pupils can progress with their learning, based on their knowledge of the learning outcomes planned by the classroom/subject teacher.'
(DfES, 2003, p12)

A growing force

The number of teaching assistants employed in schools throughout England has increased from 61,262 in 1997 to 95,815 in 2001, and looks set to continue to rise. Education Secretary Charles Clarke said in April 2003

> 'We remain committed to an expanding and improving teaching workforce – our manifesto pledged at least an extra 10,000 teachers during this Parliament. In addition, we expect that schools will employ at least 50,000 extra support staff during the same period.'

This recruitment is acknowledged as being central to the successful implementation of the School Workforce Agreement of January 2003.

References

DfES (2000) *Working with Teaching Assistants: A Good Practice Guide.* DfEE 0148/2000. London: DfES.

DfES (2001) *Professionalism and Trust – The Future of Teachers and Teaching.* A speech by the Rt Hon Estelle Morris MP to the Social Market Foundation, DfES pamphlet, November 2001. (Downloadable from www.teachernet.gov.uk, free of charge.)

DfES (2003) *Raising Standards and Tackling Workload: A National Agreement.* DfES/0172/2003. London: DfES.

Ofsted (2002) *Teaching Assistants in Primary Schools: An Evaluation of the Quality and Impact of Their Work.* HMI 434. London: Ofsted.

Top Tip

Your role has always been valued.

Remember that you are part of a team of professional adults.

Never underestimate your importance to the staff and the children of your school.

Non-teaching tasks to be delegated to support staff

- Collecting money.
- Chasing absences – teachers will need to inform the relevant member of staff when students are absent from their class or from school.
- Bulk photocopying.
- Copy typing.
- Producing standard letters – teachers may be required to contribute as appropriate in formulating the content of standard letters.
- Producing class lists – teachers may be required to be involved as appropriate in allocating students to a particular class.
- Record keeping and filing – teachers may be required to contribute to the content of records.
- Classroom display – teachers will make professional decisions in determining what material is displayed in and around their classroom.
- Analysing attendance figures – it is for teachers to make use of the outcome of analysis.
- Processing exam results – teachers will need to use the analysis of exam results.
- Collating pupil reports.
- Administering work experience – teachers may be required to support pupils on work experience (including through advice and visits).
- Administering examinations – teachers have a professional responsibility for identifying appropriate examinations for their pupils.
- Invigilating examinations.
- Administering teacher cover.
- ICT troubleshooting and minor repairs.
- Commissioning new ICT equipment.
- Ordering supplies and equipment – teachers may be involved in identifying needs.
- Stocktaking.
- Cataloguing, preparing, issuing and maintaining equipment and materials.
- Minuting meetings – teachers may be required to communicate action points from meetings.
- Coordinating and submitting bids – teachers may be required to make a professional input into the content of bids.
- Seeking and giving personnel advice.
- Managing pupil data – teachers will need to make use of the analysis of pupil data.

(DfES, 2003, pp8–9)

How to get on in your chosen career

Once you've been appointed, you will be starting on a route to improve your skills in dealing with children and adults, your knowledge of the curriculum, the routines and standards upheld by the school and your understanding of how children learn and what makes them tick.

Induction for teaching assistants

This is just the start. It will begin as soon as you've been appointed. The head will want to talk with you about a number of issues – daily routines, professional standards and conduct, managing children's behaviour and so on. The head will nominate someone from the school to be your mentor – possibly your line manager or an experienced TA. This person will guide you through the first half-term or so, until you find your feet. Always ask questions if you're not sure. No one will mind and many people will enjoy the opportunity of displaying their own wealth of knowledge.

The school will have its own induction programmes organised for all new staff members. These may vary slightly for teaching and non-teaching staff, but should contain common elements.

General induction may include

- familiarisation with the school and school site

- familiarisation with school policies immediately relevant to your role

- professional development structures

- key roles in school based on your job description

- meeting the staff team

- resource management

- child protection procedures

- health and safety considerations.

DfES induction for TAs

Part of the government's reforms has been the introduction of induction training for TAs. This more formal induction training is perhaps of most use to you when you have been in post for a short period of time. Following school-based induction, the DfES model will enable you to apply and adapt the knowledge gained in a four-day course in the context of your own school.

> 'The induction programme is an introduction to your new role and responsibilities as a teaching assistant. It identifies the skills and knowledge you will need to develop over time to become a competent practitioner.'

This DfES programme is delivered by the local education authority (LEA). Some courses have been extended to five or six days as feedback from trainers and participants has indicated that four days is not enough to cover the course content adequately.

The course modules cover

- the role and context of primary teaching assistants

- supporting literacy and numeracy

- special educational needs

- behaviour management

- English as an additional language (EAL).

National Occupational Standards for TAs

National Occupational Standards for teaching assistants were approved in 2001. A large number of qualifications have been available to teaching assistants for some time. These have varying degrees of relevance and opportunities for progression. Some are accredited to the national qualifications framework but some are not.

LEAs, schools and teaching assistants now have access to nationally recognised qualifications developed specifically for you. They provide clear progression routes into and within employment.

These NVQs (National Vocational Qualifications) are based on National Occupational Standards and are awarded when the person shows that they can do the job to these standards in the workplace. The NVQs for teaching assistants are based on the National Occupational Standards for teaching assistants that were developed by the Employers' Organisation for local government, working closely with practitioners, school managers, LEA officers and others to ensure that they reflect agreed best practice.

You may have a background in childcare, and already possess relevant qualifications for the work you are doing at the moment. You may be content to go on working with this age range, but you may want a change. If your qualifications limit you to working with a specific group of children, such as the younger children in the Foundation Stage or in Key Stage 1, you may choose to do some additional training. You will then be able to extend your experience and increase your level of expertise to work with children in Key Stage 2.

If you don't have any relevant qualifications, you can choose to study for NVQs at Levels 2 and 3. Any relevant experience you have already gained through working in schools, nurseries and so on, or any other training or qualifications you have will be taken into account when you start on an NVQ course. You will have to be able to provide evidence of this, so it's a good idea to keep any paperwork you have to show the courses you have attended recently.

If your interests lie in working with children with special educational needs or children with problems with their behaviour or their emotional and social development, there is the possibility of specialising in these roles, and parts of the NVQ optional units will be one route you can take. Other parts of the courses are suitable for any teaching assistant in any school setting.

These issues can be part of your induction programme and, later on, your performance management programme.

Level 2 NVQ

This is a useful training programme if you are new to the role of teaching assistant. You would have to study seven units in total. They cover aspects of school life and professional development, including the care and support of children, and how you can support them during their learning activities. You would find out more about the ways in which you can support your colleagues and about your part in maintaining resources and records.

You can also choose three out of five further units of work. These cover the ways in which you can support children in their literacy and numeracy activities, the contribution you can make to the use of ICT in the classroom, and how you can manage the children's behaviour, support their safety and their security, and contribute to their health and well-being.

Level 3 NVQ

If you complete the Level 2 course and want to carry on with your professional development, or if you already have qualifications to this level, you could study for the Level 3 NVQ. This is suitable for experienced teaching assistants.

There are ten units, four of which are mandatory. The units build on the areas you've already studied and the experience and expertise you've gained in your work in school.

The areas you have to study include behaviour, relationships with the children – how you can create and maintain them – and ways to support children during their learning activities. You will also be looking at your own professional practice.

The optional units are wide-ranging and include aspects of recording and assessing children's work, planning with the class teacher, and how you can support these vital activities.

There are units about children's social and emotional development, and about their health and their security. There are units that concentrate on the different ways you would support children with specific difficulties – with learning, with communication, with language and so on.

Some units will help you to gain the skills and knowledge to help children in specific areas of the curriculum, such as ICT, literacy and numeracy, or to enable all of the children to access the curriculum. And there are units to develop your own professional practice. These concentrate mainly on teamwork, on working relationships, and how to liaise with parents.

For specific details on NVQs go to www.lg-employers.gov.uk/skills/teaching/content.html

High Level Teaching Assistant

You may then choose to increase your skills to become a High Level Teaching Assistant (HLTA). This is the level you would need to have if you were to take occasional responsibility for the whole class. It will enable you to work with individual children, with small groups and with the whole class as part of the professional team. As an HLTA you would be expected to work under the supervision of the teacher, who retains overall responsibility for the children and their learning. You would, however, work with a greater level of autonomy than a teaching assistant is usually expected to exercise.

The head of the school will identify the sorts of activities for which, and the times when you could be expected to take the whole class, and when you

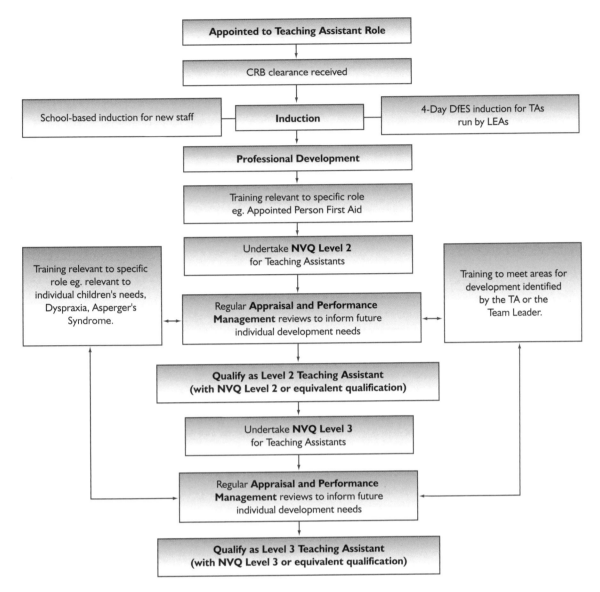

```
        Appointed to Teaching Assistant Role
                        │
              CRB clearance received
                        │
┌──────────────────┐    ┌───────────┐    ┌──────────────────────┐
│ School-based     ├────┤ Induction ├────┤ 4-Day DfES induction │
│ induction for    │    │           │    │ for TAs              │
│ new staff        │    │           │    │ run by LEAs          │
└──────────────────┘    └───────────┘    └──────────────────────┘
                        │
              Professional Development
                        │
          Training relevant to specific role
            eg. Appointed Person First Aid
                        │
               Undertake NVQ Level 2
                for Teaching Assistants
                        │
┌────────────────┐   Regular Appraisal and Performance   ┌────────────────┐
│ Training       │   Management reviews to inform future  │ Training to    │
│ relevant to    ├──▶ individual development needs    ◀───┤ meet areas for │
│ specific role  │                                        │ development    │
└────────────────┘                                        └────────────────┘
                        │
          Qualify as Level 2 Teaching Assistant
        (with NVQ Level 2 or equivalent qualification)
                        │
               Undertake NVQ Level 3
                for Teaching Assistants
                        │
               Regular Appraisal and Performance
               Management reviews to inform future
                    individual development needs
                        │
          Qualify as Level 3 Teaching Assistant
        (with NVQ Level 3 or equivalent qualification)
```

From appointment to NVQ Level 3

would need to work alongside a qualified teacher. For example, there are strict guidelines about who can supervise children during PE lessons because of the potential for accidents, but you may be a qualified football coach. Decisions will always rest with the head of the school, who will take into account your expertise, your competency and the nature of the children in the class.

HLTA standards

The standards you need to demonstrate in order to be recognised as an HLTA are organised into three sections.

1 Professional values and practice.

2 Knowledge and understanding.

3 Teaching and learning activities.

1 Professional values and practice

These standards are concerned with the development of professional attitudes and the expected level of commitment which, as a candidate for HLTA, you will have to give to the role.

2 Knowledge and understanding

These standards reflect the need for the HLTA to be able to work as a member of a professional team with teachers. As an HLTA you will have to demonstrate that you have the knowledge, expertise and awareness of the children's curriculum to do this. You would also be expected to be able to demonstrate that you know how to use your skills, expertise and experience as you support children's learning.

3 Teaching and learning activities

As an HLTA you must show that you can work effectively '...under the professional direction and supervision of a qualified teacher' (DfES and TTA, 2003). You would have to be able to contribute to a range of teaching and learning and pastoral activities in your subjects or areas of expertise. As an HLTA you must be able to use your skills for planning, monitoring, assessment and class management.

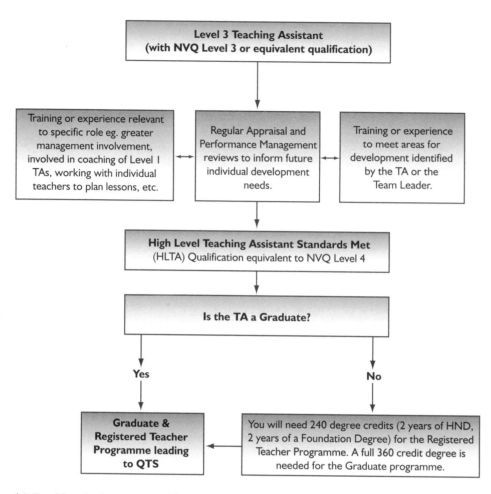

Level 3 Teaching Assistant
(with NVQ Level 3 or equivalent qualification)

Training or experience relevant to specific role eg. greater management involvement, involved in coaching of Level I TAs, working with individual teachers to plan lessons, etc.

Regular Appraisal and Performance Management reviews to inform future individual development needs.

Training or experience to meet areas for development identified by the TA or the Team Leader.

High Level Teaching Assistant Standards Met
(HLTA) Qualification equivalent to NVQ Level 4

Is the TA a Graduate?

Yes

No

Graduate & Registered Teacher Programme leading to QTS

You will need 240 degree credits (2 years of HND, 2 years of a Foundation Degree) for the Registered Teacher Programme. A full 360 credit degree is needed for the Graduate programme.

Level 3 Teaching Assistant to Qualified Teacher Status

HLTA training

The training for this is at a level equivalent to Level 4 NVQ, but will take account of any prior experience you have and any qualifications you already possess. There is information about the qualifications you need on the HLTA website at www.hlta.gov.uk. Remember, that you need to be able to demonstrate that you have achieved the standards up to Level 3 before you undertake this training.

Your first task is to secure funding through your local education authority [LEA]. Talk to your head about how to go about this. Once funding is agreed you have to find a training provider and apply for a place with them. From April 2004 to September 2005 there will be 36 providers of training for aspiring HLTAs. These include universities, colleges, schools, education authorities and some private firms. If you go to www.hlta.gov.uk and follow the links to 'training and assessment' and then 'training providers' you will find instructions for locating your nearest provider and an online application form.

If you would like a copy of 'Meeting the standards: a guide to higher level training and assessment' you can order this, free of charge, by telephoning 0845 606 0323 or sending an email to ttapublications@dforcegroup.com

From HLTA to Qualified Teacher Status (QTS)

Having got this far in your professional development, you may want to consider training to become a teacher.

You should have a degree already. If not, you may need to do this as the next step. There are several options for how you go about this, which you can explore with your head or your training provider, to find the best way for you.

The intention of the DfES to make the transition from HLTA to QTS possible is underlined by the fact that in 2002/2003, 100 places on the employment-based route towards QTS were reserved for teaching assistants.

References

Teachernet (2003) www.teachernet.gov.uk/ professionaldevelopment

www.hlta.gov.uk

www.lg-employers.gov.uk

How am I getting on?

Performance management (PM) is the process by which you, and the headteacher, find out how much progress you have made – professionally speaking – over the year. It is an opportunity to review new experiences, and identify the new skills and levels of knowledge and understanding you have gained. It is a time to reflect, to think about how far you have come and to put into words where you want to go to next. This decision will be a shared one.

Teaching assistants working within teams, with clearly defined development objectives under the line management of a senior teacher, are becoming an increasingly common feature of many primary schools. You should reasonably expect to receive some form of performance management that is in line with your role and your responsibilities.

The aims of performance management are to

- provide an opportunity for a two-way dialogue and review
- add value to your role
- plan for professional development
- recognise and celebrate achievements
- identify any areas of weakness
- set achievable targets
- identify training needs.

Performance management structure

Many schools now operate a model of line management like the one shown below. This places you as part of the Special Needs Team under the management of the special needs coordinator (SENCO).

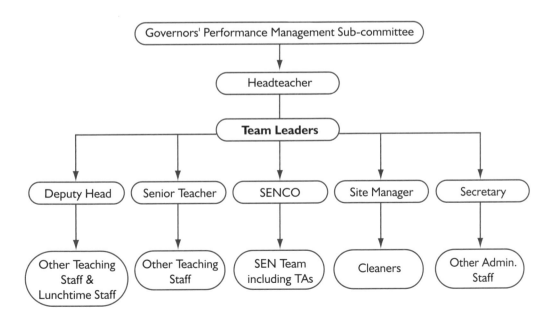

Performance management chain of responsibility

Making performance management work

Performance management is a real opportunity to affirm the value that a school places on both the role of TAs in general and the part played by an individual. It can reinforce the professional nature of your position in the school, recognising achievements and setting targets for the future. It should underline the importance that an individual's contribution makes to the success of the team, and consequently the learning outcomes for children throughout the school.

A professional review of everyone's work is required in order to further develop individual strengths and weaknesses and to meet the strategic needs of the school as a whole.

The performance management review is an opportunity for you to access accredited training programmes such as NVQ Level 2 or 3. This performance management process should build upon the continuous dialogue between you and your line manager, offering a formal opportunity for you to discuss your performance and professional needs. These reviews should be conducted in an honest, open and professional manner.

The process of performance management

Meetings through the year

Regular meetings organised by the team leader with the teaching assistant team provide the chance for informal feedback on general issues regarding the TAs' roles and priorities within the school, an opportunity to share successes or concerns and a chance for the team to re-evaluate priorities in the short term.

Observations of TAs

Observations of teachers in classrooms are now a well-established part of the monitoring and self-evaluation aspects of school life. Although few of us enjoy being watched carrying out our job, it can be a very affirming experience. Indeed, where observations are carried out in a culture of professionalism, trust and mutual respect, they are a key ingredient in the recipe for school improvement and staff development.

The observation of teaching assistants in supporting the work of a whole class, group or individual is less common than that of teachers, but it is no less valuable. It helps to inform and affirm your continuous professional development and leads into the formal performance management process.

As with all observations, a clear focus should be agreed between the TA and the observer in advance. It is likely that this focus will be derived from the existing performance management targets that you agreed to. You will need to pre-arrange a time, an activity, the group of children you will be working with and what the observer is looking for. For example, if one of your targets for this year is to develop strategies and expertise in dealing with children who can't concentrate on their work, then you may choose to work with a group including at least one such child. The observer will be noting how you react to that child when their attention starts to wander and what you do to re-attract their interest. The observer will want to see what you do if the child starts to disrupt the group.

After the observation you will be able to talk through what you did, and discuss any alternative strategies you could have taken. You will have time to reflect on what you did and how well you did it.

Mid-term review

Where performance management cycles cover an extended period of an academic or calendar year, it is often valuable for team leaders to hold a mid-term review. For example, if the formal performance management cycle begins in April, a mid-term review in September or October allows priorities to be re-assessed and progress with targets to be measured informally. This has the effect of focusing the minds of the team leader and yourself on the objectives for the remaining two terms of the cycle.

Self-review

Prior to any formal meeting you should have an opportunity to reflect on your own performance against targets previously set, consider your achievements and identify any areas you feel need

to be developed, or that you would like to develop. This self-review often helps to provide a sharp focus for the formal meeting and encourages you to reflect upon your work during the year.

There should be regular informal dialogue between you and your team leader throughout the period between reviews that will provide a basis for the formal meetings.

The formal meeting

This meeting should be scheduled far enough in advance to allow you time to complete the self-review process and for the team leader to consider the following.

- To what extent targets established in the last appraisal (or appointment in the case of first appraisals) have been met.

- The self-review by the person appraised.

- Observations on performance of the person appraised by the line manager.

The agenda for this meeting may well include the following items.

- Highlighting successes and achievements since the last formal meeting.

- A discussion of the areas that could be considered for development as part of the targets to be set. These should include a reference to school and team targets.

- Setting of targets for achievement by the next appraisal. These could well include pupil progress targets for individuals or groups with whom you work.

- Agreed competencies, or what performance will look like when done well.

- Consideration of job description and agreement on changes if necessary.

- Setting a date for the mid-term review.

The outcome

At the end of the meeting there should be an agreement between you on the basic structure of the performance management review statement and action plan.

The statement should contain three to five targets for you to work towards, a summary of the strengths, successes and areas for development. Both forms will then be formally completed by the team leader and passed to you for approval in an agreed timescale.

The agreed final statement should be signed by both of you, and you will each keep a copy.

> **Top Tip**
>
> Performance management is your opportunity to talk about yourself – your achievements, your successes and your aspirations.
>
> Take it and use it. Enjoy spending time on yourself for a change!

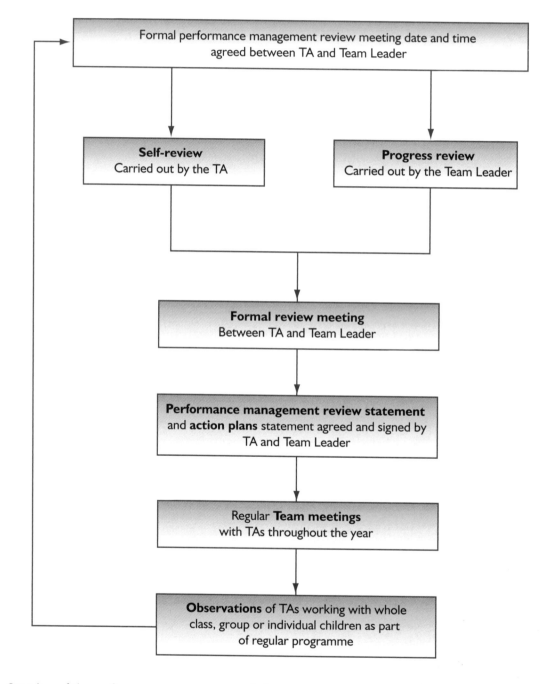

Overview of the performance management path for TAs

Working with children – the legal aspects

Everyone who works with children has a duty to have the welfare of the child at the heart of everything they do. There are laws that define what you can and can't do. There are local regulations that uphold that law and provide specific guidelines for you to follow. If you step outside these laws you can expect serious repercussions.

It is the duty of the school to provide you with all the information you need to keep yourself safe and to protect the children in your care. It is your responsibility to

● read that material

● attend any necessary training

● follow the guidelines at all times.

Behaviour management

The school will have its own set of guidelines on managing child behaviour both in and out of the classroom. Successful behaviour management policies are those that set clear expectations for all those who work in the school. These policies are reflected in the practice that creates commonly acknowledged boundaries between acceptable and unacceptable behaviours. They will set out clear sanctions for those who make inappropriate choices about their own behaviour and reward those who make the correct choices.

Your role within the behaviour management code should be explicit within the policy and the practice. On a whole-school level, all teaching assistants must be clear about what is expected of them in dealing with challenging behaviour both within and outside of the classroom situation.

Within each classroom the class teacher should involve you as well as the children in establishing ground rules for dealing with the behaviour of individual children, or for addressing general concerns. There is a real chance of conflict if you attempt to impose your expectations on a class without reference to the class teacher. Equally, if you are excluded from taking any responsibility within the classroom, you may well feel undervalued or disaffected.

A clear behaviour management policy and school ethos go a long way towards establishing common expectations throughout the school. However, responsibility for the learning in the classroom rests with the class teacher. Effective class teachers will lead this responsibility, while empowering you to help them meet their goals at the same time.

Making the almost impossible look easy

All adults who work within our schools find themselves in difficult situations from time to time. This is an inevitable consequence of working with people either as groups or individuals. While school sweatshirts may give all children a common appearance, we have to acknowledge that as individuals they are all inherently different. Their lives and experiences before walking through the school gates each morning will remain hidden from us for the most part. We are right to expect that all children meet our school's commonly agreed expectations in terms of behaviour and courtesy, but we live in an imperfect world and some of this imperfection is only too real for the young people we work with each day.

To witness experienced staff, either teachers or teaching assistants, being able to defuse a potentially threatening situation with a parent, remaining calm and focused when confronted by a child who is being uncooperative in the extreme, and – perhaps most impressive of all – connecting with a child who appears to be unreachable, is an inspiring sight for those who are new to the school team.

Ask the member of staff how they made the difficult situation look so easy and they may not be able to tell you. Some may feel that it is a result of experience, common sense and the fact that they have developed a strong relationship with the child in the past. Others may feel that the key is appearing to remain calm when all around them is chaos, never meeting fire with fire. For others the secret is to make sure that the child or adult knows that they can trust you to be fair, consistent and not lose faith in them as people when the situation returns to normal.

The truth is that skilled teachers and teaching assistants use combinations of some or all of these qualities, often unconsciously. What they all share is a desire to do what is best for that child. Most importantly, through day-to-day dealings with the adult, the child knows that this is the case.

Although dealing with difficult situations is one of the great challenges that staff in schools face, it can also be one of the most rewarding aspects of the role. The important work that will enable you to deal with challenging issues is done when the world is calm, when you can take the time and trouble to get to know the children and to create trust and respect within them.

Physical restraint

The school should have a clear policy on the use of physical restraint with children. This is a complicated area and one that is certainly more grey than it is black and white. In extreme cases, which, while rare, do occur, you or a teacher might find yourselves in a position where you are tempted to physically restrain a child to prevent them causing injury to themselves, to others or to property. Before doing so, you should be clear that the school's policy authorises you to take this action, and it is equally important that you are familiar with the strict guidelines on the use of physical restraint.

You should be aware that these guidelines often contain the phrase

> 'no more than the minimum necessary force should be used and the teaching assistant should seek to avoid causing injury to the pupil'.

This is clearly open to interpretation and challenge at a later date. It seems unreasonable to expect any member of staff to place themselves in this dangerous position without significant levels of training. Even then, the decision to use the authorisation granted by the head must be an individual one.

What the law says

The Education Act 1997 clarified the position about the use of physical force by teachers, and others authorised by the headteacher, to control or restrain children. The clarification was made by adding a section (Section 550A) to the Education Act 1996.

This new section came into force on 1 September 1998 and applies to all schools. It restates principles derived from common law and statute that have, in the past, been misunderstood.

- Where necessary, reasonable force can be used to control or restrain children.

- Physical contact with children may also be appropriate or necessary in other circumstances.

Teaching assistants authorised by the headteacher, who have control or charge of children, are allowed to use reasonable force to prevent a child from

- committing a crime, including behaving in a way that would be an offence if the child were not under the age of criminal responsibility

- causing injury to themselves or others

- causing damage to property including their own

- causing serious disruption, to the extent that good order and discipline could not be maintained.

This is only applicable when an authorised person is on the school premises, or has lawful control or charge of the child concerned on an authorised out-of-school activity.

There is no legal definition of reasonable force. The degree and reasonableness of force will depend upon the circumstances in which force is used.

Everyone has the right to defend themselves against an attack provided they do not use a disproportionate degree of force to do so.

> **Top Tip**
>
> Make sure that you are familiar with the school's policy on handling and restraint. If you do have to intervene, do so with extreme care. Remember everything that happened and write it down as soon as you can.

Staff protection

The overwhelming majority of us who work with young people in schools do so because we believe we are making a positive difference to their lives, through either academic or personal development, and we want them to have opportunities as they move into adulthood. The knowledge that anyone would consciously harm a child either physically or mentally is both abhorrent and unthinkable. Taken one step further, to be accused of harming a child in any way is every teacher or teaching assistant's worst nightmare.

However remote the threat of an accusation being made about a member of staff might appear to be, it has happened and will continue to happen. All staff need to be mindful of the risks they take in

working with young people, especially where this work is carried out on a one-to-one basis.

We cannot entirely remove these risks but we can ensure that we minimise them. If you feel uneasy about a situation, you should alert your line manager or colleague to this concern. Always work with the door open if you are expected to be in a separate room or ensure that the work takes place in a common area. If the concerns remain, do continue to communicate these worries to a line manager or senior colleague and, if necessary, request a change of child.

Physical contact

Following on from the last point about self-protection, the need to avoid physical contact with children in our schools is clear and well documented. It is unnecessary and unrealistic to suggest that you should only touch children in emergencies. Particularly with younger children, touching them is inevitable and can give welcome reassurance to the child. However, you should bear in mind that even perfectly innocent actions can sometimes be misconstrued. It is important for us to be sensitive to a child's reaction to physical contact and to act appropriately.

For example, if you have to change the clothes of a child who has had an accident, ask the child to remove the soiled clothing themselves. If the child is unable to do this, ask them if they mind if you remove it for them. If they don't want you to do this, offer them the privacy of changing in a separate place such as the toilet cubicle. In some circumstances you may even need to call the child's parent.

If you have any concerns that your actions may be misconstrued, it is essential that you report the incident to the headteacher or your line manager.

Confidentiality

Many of our schools could be classed as fitting into the 'small workplace' category. It is not always possible to keep all information that is passed between staff to those adults who are directly involved in a situation. What is essential is that whatever knowledge about a child or a family any adult in the school holds, you must respect the confidential nature of this information.

If you live within the school's own community, this can place you in a potentially difficult or embarrassing position. It may well be that you are privy to information relating to a child who lives next door to you, or know something about the family life of an adult you regularly see socially. It may also be that parents who know you well feel that you will be able to exert some influence over the class within which their child will be placed, or that you can resolve a friendship problem their child is experiencing.

This is not an easy situation to resolve, and explains why many teachers are keen to live away from the area in which they work. In order to deal with these issues you must remember that you have a professional position to maintain and you should give loyalty to, and expect it from, other members of the team.

Confidentiality can mean not passing on information about the child's progress to their parents unless the teacher has specifically asked you to give such a message. In those circumstances you would be speaking as 'Mrs A, the teaching assistant and member of the school professional team', not as 'Jan from next door'. It can mean not telling a parent that their child was hit in the face by George at playtime, or that her daughter was told off for not getting on with her work. If you see the results of tests or know which classes the children are going into in September, or that Miss D is leaving in August, you must keep it quiet until it is made public by the headteacher at the time that they deem to be best.

Children tell you things all the time. Some talk a lot and some very little. Some seem to say only things that are important to them and others seem to chat far more generally. Mostly, what they say doesn't have serious implications. However, occasionally a child will pass on something that affects their welfare and their ability to learn. You need to spot this and you may need to act on it.

Your relationship with children is not one of equality. It is important for children to realise that anything they say becomes open to your interpretation. They must realise that you are bound by the professional ethic to look after their welfare.

things for you to remember if this ever happens to you. Firstly, you must not question the child. Just say something like 'Thank you for telling me.'

Secondly, the child must be told that the information is not confidential and that you will have to tell someone. 'I'm going to have to tell … what you just told me.'

In this situation, what you have been told has to be passed on to your child protection officer. You may not, however, tell anyone else. Not the class teacher, not your friend, not your partner – no one else must know.

Remember, all information is confidential to someone. You have to decide what to do with what you are told, but where there is a policy or procedure you must follow it.

There should be the opportunity for all staff to have access to up-to-date child protection training either within school or through an external provider. Through the performance management reviews you could request support or training on child protection issues.

Dealing with a child protection concern is fraught with difficulty on both a personal and an administrative level. It can become deeply upsetting to witness a child who we believe to be the victim of abuse, violence or neglect. On the other side of the coin, we need to be very careful not to ask questions of a child that are in any way leading, or will place them or us in a difficult position later on.

In addition, many adults are naturally concerned about making referrals that are based on false assumptions and triggering a chain of reactions that quickly escalate beyond their control, resulting in social services or police involvement. While this is a genuine fear for many people, the child protection policy in schools and with external agencies should be robust and balanced enough to ensure that all referrals are dealt with in an appropriate and fair-minded way.

Part of this is also the development of trust. There is a difference between using what you discover to further the interests and well-being of the child and simply spreading gossip. The child must realise that they have given you the information in trust and that you will use it if you need to.

Confidentiality is, however, a strange thing in that information is always confidential to some people and not to others.

A classic example of this comes with the child protection procedures. Your school will have a laid-down procedure, which you must follow. If you don't know what it is, find out now!

Child protection

One of the most disturbing issues faced by school staff on an alarmingly regular basis is linked to concerns about an individual child's failure to thrive for a multitude of possible reasons.

Your school will have both a child protection policy and an appointed child protection officer. It is vital that all staff in the school are both familiar with the policy and aware of their role within it on a practical level. The policy may well make specific reference to the role of teaching assistants.

Because of the regular individual and group work you carry out, teaching assistants are arguably in a stronger position than class teachers to identify symptoms of abuse or neglect. Be sure that you know who to turn to if you have any concerns, what you should do and what you should not do.

Part of this procedure will cover what you have to do if a child tells you something that makes you worry about their welfare. There are two vital

> **Top Tip**
>
> The child protection procedure is very important. Your school has a laid-down procedure that you must follow. Make sure you have a copy and that you could follow it if you had to. Most importantly, you must know the name of your child protection officer as well as what to do if that person is not available to you.

Being a professional

Towards a definition

'I get paid from 9.00 to 3.30. I don't get paid for lunch. The pay is really poor and now they expect me to stay to a staff meeting. What a cheek!'

Is this how you feel? If it is, then you are in the wrong mindset.

You joined a profession and the profession assumes that you want to be a part of it. It makes that assumption because you turn up for work.

There has almost certainly been a time, late one evening or during a weekend, when you started to think about George. You may have considered how he had behaved or what he did, or what you did, or what he is doing, or what you are going to do next, or… You didn't just think about it, you worked out what you would do about it, too. Be honest, it has happened. Nobody paid you for it and nobody made you do it. But you did it anyway. Why? Because you're a professional.

It goes with the territory, just like following the restraint guidelines or the child protection procedure. You have to act in the best interest of the children you work with. They expect you to behave as a professional. They expect you to care about them. Sometimes, this means you have to go the extra mile.

The system has to play fair with you, too. If there is an item on the staff meeting that matters to you, it should be taken first so that you can go when it is covered. It shouldn't be assumed that you are always available. It should be accepted that you would attend only when it is critical to your work. Efforts should be made to accommodate the routine within your working day. You should respond to the unusual or the exceptional.

In a particular primary school, there is a whole-school assembly taken by the headteacher on a Friday afternoon. It is a celebration assembly where children share their successes of the week. Parents are invited to share the celebration. During the assembly each teacher meets with their assistants and plans the lessons for the following week. The school has made the effort to accommodate the planning routine into the assistants' normal working hours.

The same school has staff meetings every other week on a Tuesday, after school. Occasionally, the agenda includes an item that the assistants need to know. Last time this happened it concerned an

urgent and important discussion about a particular incident of bullying. The item was put first and given a maximum of 15 minutes. Assistants were invited with 48 hours' notice. It was the only time that it had happened in that term. The school had 14 assistants at the time. Nobody made them go to the meeting and they were neither blackmailed to attend nor threatened if they didn't. However, the assistants felt they were a part of the team. They considered themselves to be professionals. At the meeting the item was taken first and actually took 12 minutes to cover. At the end of the item, the assistants were thanked for coming and given time to withdraw. Fourteen professionals left the room.

Professionalism is a two-way process. If you behave like a professional, you will be treated like one. You are part of a privileged world. It is the world that is privileged to shape future generations. It is a world that knows that the future is in your hands. So, do a professional job and, if something is not to your liking, make a professional response.

You have a right to a contract. You have a right to a job description. You have a right to a reasonable wage. But you are a professional. So, deal with it as a professional.

> **Top Tip**
>
> You are a professional the day you start work. Now you need to think like one. The best way is to act like a professional. Now everyone else will see you as one. They will then make you feel like a professional.

Loyalty and whistle-blowing

We all have groups of people we feel comfortable with. They may even be friends. We may be working with people we have known for a long time. They may be in a senior position to us. For you, these groups or individuals may include the other assistants, the teachers or the headteacher.

We must accept that we are all part of the same team. As a member of that team we owe loyalty to the rest of the team. We stand by them and support their decisions as if they were our own. To anyone outside the team, we appear as a single, strong force.

Most of the time you will be able to work alongside these people without a problem. But every now and then, you may come across someone who makes you feel uncomfortable. It may be because of some of the things they say. It may be because of some of the things they do.

We are all different and the behaviour of other team members is going to take some getting used to. Sometimes, however, you may have a bigger issue. This could be for one of two main reasons.

Firstly, you may find yourself at odds with the direction taken by the rest of the team. It's not that they are wrong, just different. In this situation you have three choices. You can try to get them to see things your way, you can do things their way, or you can leave. In the end, the strength of the team is what decides how well it does the job. Your work should make the team stronger. If your effect is to weaken the team, you should try to adjust to the way that the others are working.

Secondly, you may discover that one member of the team is working against the interests of the rest of the team – they may even be acting illegally. If so, then this is where you blow the whistle. Any underhand or illegal act must be dealt with. Ask if you can talk in confidence to the headteacher. The head will listen, advise and help you to deal with the situation in an acceptable and professional way. They will take the matter further if that is what is needed to resolve the situation.

Top Tip

The team is there to support the children. A strong team does a better job than a weak one. Help to make your team stronger. But if you find someone who is acting against children's interests then you must report it.

You should never cover up an illegal act.

Being a member of the team

Teamwork is when your job interlaces with the jobs being done by other adults at the time. This is most noticeable in whole-class situations.

The teacher usually leads the session (although there is no rule that says that they have to) and the other adults need to be clear about what their role will be in this situation. The possibilities include

- discipline
- encouragement
- modelling
- summary
- assessment.

These possible roles are not equal. If the discipline is not right, then no learning will take place. Discipline has to be established and it must come first. Encouragement and modelling should be a way of life. Summary is not always possible but assessment is. So when you can think of no other role to fulfil, assess!

Discipline

The mildest possible form of discipline is a glance. The look is next, then the long look and then the stare. Discipline measures grow in small steps. It is important to know all the steps that are available and then use them all. The table below is drawn in three columns. Start at the top of the left column and move down each column in turn. The first column is just facial expression, the second adds movements of the arm and hand, and the last adds sound and body movement as well. As you move through the stages you become more and more disruptive.

Each of us has a different list. Your list will contain those actions that you are comfortable with. You can add the things that you do to the table, and cross off the things that you don't do. If you end up with very few things, then you lack flexibility. If you have too many, then the children will be confused as to what each means. Getting the balance right is as important as making sure that you use each consistently, keep the order the same and that each always means the same thing.

FACIAL EXPRESSION	ARM AND HEAD	SOUND AND BODY
The glance	One small head shake	A small cough
The look	Several head shakes	'Sshhh!'
The long look	Finger to lips with small arm movement	Whispered name
The stare		Stated name
One eyebrow	Vigorous head shake	Shouted name
Two eyebrows	Finger to lips with large arm movement	Move to child
The frown		Move child
The grimace		Forcible extraction while shouting
The screwed-up face		

What you will want to achieve is minimum disruption and maximum effect, so it is important that you know what is on your list and use it carefully. If you start too far into the list, you are not giving the child a fair chance. Remember, you know a child's behaviour is improving when you can get the desired effect at an earlier stage on your list. If you don't know what's on your list and where you start each time with a particular child, how will you know they are getting better? How will you be able to give them a chance to improve?

Discipline becomes far more effective when a shared approach is used. This means that all the adults in the session use the same list and that the elements on the list are kept in the same order. It is also important that each element always means the same thing – consistency matters!

The other intriguing thing about discipline is that it is dependent on eye contact. If you don't have eye contact, you have to establish it first and this forces you into the third column of the table. It means you will be disruptive. It means you will have to start doing all the things that the children are not allowed to do, like talking, like moving, like nudging. If the children are not allowed to do it then neither should you as far as possible. Worse still, you are going to make all the children look at you and stop looking where they are supposed to be looking – at the teacher.

The only solution is to make sure that you have eye contact with all the children – just like the teacher. The only place that you will get eye contact is to be where the teacher is. The teacher is at the front.

Get to the front. Now you have eye contact. Now you can be effective.

Now you are part of the team.

> **Top Tip**
>
> A child who is involved is not disruptive. When children get restless or distracted, they look for other things to do. Some children don't try to distract others while some will try to involve peers in an alternative activity. When all the children are fully involved, discipline is not a problem.
>
> **Try to involve all the children.**

Encouragement

There is Sarah, sitting on the mat just dying to join in. But Sarah is shy. You can see by her face that there is something she wants to say but she never quite plucks up enough courage. You could ignore her or you could try to get her involved. Suppose you decide to involve her. What could you do? A smile and nod may help. For some children, you may have to ask them.

In fact there is a whole list of things you could do. You have just seen a list of ways to discipline. You can also make a list of the ways that you can encourage a child to participate. It is also in three columns. It also becomes more disruptive as you move through the stages.

Each of us has our own list. Try writing yours. If you get stuck, ask someone to help you. The children will be able to help because they will know what you do. When you have finished, you need to ask the same questions as before. Is it too long? Is it too short? Is it used consistently?

Remember, once you know the list exists you can use it as a measure of how much better a child is at participating. It will only work if you start at an earlier point in the list than the point that evoked a response last time. Only this way can you identify that a child is making progress.

Unsurprisingly, encouragement also needs eye contact. The only place that you will get eye contact is to be where the teacher is. The teacher is at the front.

Get to the front. Now you have eye contact. Now you can be effective.

Now you are part of the team.

> **Top Tip**
>
> Children won't necessarily know what your signs of encouragement mean. So tell them before you use the signs. Either take them to one side and explain or, every time you use the sign, say or mouth the meaning and remember to be consistent – one sign has one meaning.
>
> **Teach the meaning of your signs.**

Modelling

Imagine you are ten and I've just dumped you in a classroom for the first time. Not a problem? I forgot to mention that the classroom is in Spain. How's your Spanish?

More to the point, how would you know what you were expected to do? You could just follow everyone else, but that doesn't mean you will be doing the right thing. You could watch the teacher, but they give the instructions, they don't follow them. You could watch the assistant. A good assistant will always model the appropriate behaviour. They will show you how it is done.

Modelling is particularly important for children who don't understand English. It's equally important for children who are not used to the school environment, in the Foundation Stage, for example. In both cases it shows children the way to behave. It tells them what is safe, what is acceptable.

Modelling is also reassuring for children. It both establishes the values you uphold and demonstrates that the values are consistent. It can show children how different situations can bend the rules. For example, it gives the children permission to cheer the efforts of a peer and also tells them when the cheering has to stop.

Modelling goes on all the time. Any time a child can see you, in or out of school, they will see what you do as a model of what is acceptable. You are teaching by example. It doesn't matter whether it's in the high street or the corridor, the school library or the public library, the school hall or the cinema. You are a model of good practice. It is all part of being a professional.

Sometimes you won't know that you are being observed while at others you will want to be seen. If you want to be seen, make sure you are where you can be seen – just like the teacher. Perhaps the only place that you can be sure you can be seen is to be where the teacher is. If the teacher is at the front, get to the front. Now you have eye contact. Now you can be effective.

Now you are part of the team.

> **Top Tip**
>
> If you find yourself about to tell a child off, ask yourself how they should have known that their action was wrong. Instead of telling them off, remind them of the signs they should have looked for that could have told the child that their behaviour was wrong. If you can't find any, then perhaps you are at fault for not ensuring the reminders were there. Children need to be told what works instead of what they shouldn't do.
>
> **Catch someone doing it right!**
>
> **Celebrate success publicly.**

Summarising

It was literacy time. We were all sitting on the mat watching the teacher and the assistant sitting next to her. Fishing behind her with one hand, the teacher produced the big book. It was *The Hungry Caterpillar*. We all waited in eager anticipation, all eyes glued to the book cover.

Now, if you know the book you will know that there is a caterpillar that is about to eat everything in sight. Each day of the week this caterpillar embarks on a new feast. And that was the key point. The learning objective for the session was that the children would know the days of the week in the correct order.

Off we go. The teacher takes us to each new day for a new meal. We pretend to be the caterpillar crawling round the mat and then we all stop and look at the imaginary fruit of the day and then we pretend to eat it. We chomp our way through everything in sight. The teacher has an exciting way of reading and we make the most of our dramatic skills. We are having fun, lots of fun!

So much fun, in fact, that we are losing sight of the learning objective. Or are we? No, not in this session. The assistant has a whiteboard and a marker pen. Every time the teacher says the next day of the week for the first time, the assistant adds it to the list that grows on the whiteboard.

Isn't it a distraction? Too right it is! It is supposed to be. After all, it is the learning objective – the most important aspect of the lesson.

This is 'summary' – and it is also good practice. The assistant is summarising the key points of the

session for all to see. Summary is a skill that has to be taught and this technique shows the children how it is done.

Of course, it isn't just summary. The assistant was careful to model the handwriting style that was being used in the class. Each time she wrote on the board, she first put the board on her lap. She then carefully modelled the correct writing style and then held it up for all to see. This was a further example of good practice.

The thing that made this episode exceptional was what happened after the story had finished. The teacher split the class into groups for follow-up activities based on the days of the week. The groups were organised by ability and the assistant was working with the least able group. She took her group to their work area for their task. It was to write a poem where each line started with a day of the week. The assistant took the board with her, thus creating a link between the two parts of the lesson. The children now had a context for the words. The assistant had created continuity of learning by linking the task to a previous experience. Brilliant!

Summary only works if the children can see you do it. The only place you can go where you can guarantee this is to be where the teacher is. The teacher is at the front.

Get to the front. Now you have eye contact. Now you can be effective.

Now you are part of the team.

> **Top Tip**
>
> It's a whole-class session and you know what is going to happen and what the teacher wants the children to learn. Now ask yourself whether the learning objective might get lost in the activity. Can you identify the key words or phrases that are critical to the session? If you can, talk to the teacher about how you want to do it. Prepare any resources in advance of the session. Practise before the session so that you know it works.
>
> **Be thorough in your preparation.**
> **Practise first.**

Assessment

The children are all involved and behaving well. This is a session where summary is not needed and everyone knows what to do and what is expected. You still have a job to do. It is called assessment.

Education is about learning things. Learning is what distinguishes education from child-minding.

The teacher starts with a list of things children have to learn. Learning is in three areas – knowledge, understanding and skills.

- *Knowledge* is about facts.

- *Understanding* is about comprehension, perception, awareness, and insight.

- *Skills* are how well you can do something.

The teacher has to choose what the children need to learn next. The decision will be based on what the children did last and how well they got on. It will also draw on sequences that are laid down in guidance documents both locally and nationally. From all of this, the teacher ends up with the one thing they want the children to learn at 2.00pm on Tuesday. This becomes the learning objective.

The teacher now has to think of a way to teach this one thing. They will want to make sure that the method is appropriate, that the resources are available, that the work is at the right level and that it is the best way they can think of doing it. They now work out how to organise the room and the children. They sort out what needs doing in advance and devise strategies for anything that might go wrong. They also have 'Plan B' ready in

case the lesson is not possible for some reason beyond their control. Finally, a good teacher will test the session in their mind. Will it be fun? Will they enjoy it? Am I looking forward to it?

At 2.00pm on Tuesday, the activity happens. Learning takes place.

But, who learned what? That is the purpose of assessment. Remember, the activity was devised to teach a particular thing. That is the only thing that can be assessed with any confidence. After all, a lot of things might happen, but the activity will deliver the learning objective.

So you know what you are looking for. The objective may be 'to know the 3 times table' or 'to recognise the relationship between relative speed and sound' or 'to use the principles of least waste to mark out a piece of material ready for cutting'.

Now pick the children you want to assess. Allow sufficient time for each – five minutes per child per objective is a good guide.

With the objective and the child in clear focus, you now make the assessment. Does George know his 3 times table?

As soon as you make the assessment, record the evidence. Don't leave it until later on, do it now. If you don't, then you will forget. Imagine, you do the assessment then take your group for a different task. You have to see to other children during the morning break and then you have to look after a child who is ill. After doing supervision

GEORGE				TUESDAY 2.00PM					
1 x 3	2 x 3	3 x 3	4 x 3	5 x 3	6 x 3	7 x 3	8 x 3	9 x 3	10 x 3
	✓✓✓	✓✓✓	✓✓✓	✓✓✓	✓✗✓	✗✓✓		✗✗✗	✓✓✓

at lunchtime, you accompany a group strolling around the field looking for bugs. You now have to help a disabled child at PE and you finally collapse in the staff room ten minutes after the end of school. At this point someone asks you if George knows his 3 times table.

You might say, 'Yes, I think so … Yes, I'm sure he did.' Or, you might say, 'He got each right three times except 6 x 3 and 7 x 3, which were both wrong once, and 9 x 3, which he could not do at all from memory and his count-on strategy did not work because of his uncertainty with 6 x 3 and 7 x 3. 8 x 3 and 1 x 3 were not tested.'

The only way you will be able to make the second statement is if you have kept a record at the time. The record could have looked like the one on p25.

A record like this highlights the child's area of weakness as well as a fault in the activity (not using 8 x 3 as a stepping stone to 9 x 3). It also contains no words and is easy to interpret at a glance. These are two key principles in a good record. After all, you won't have time to write anything and no one is ever likely to read it if you do. The record contains all the necessary information as it stands.

So the key ingredients of good assessment are

- knowing the objective

- knowing who you will assess

- having the record prepared ready

- not using words in a record

- making the record as you do the assessment.

Another essential ingredient is eye contact. You will need to see their face. It will tell you whether they know or not. In a whole-class session you will need to have eye contact with all the children – just like the teacher. The only place that you will get eye contact is to be where the teacher is. The teacher is at the front. Get to the front. Now you have eye contact. Now you can be effective.

Now you are part of the team.

Top Tip

It's a whole-class session and you have chosen two children to assess. You know the objective and have designed the sheet for the record. Now, make sure the two children are sitting next to each other and in your line of sight. If they are not together and not in line of sight then you may miss the signs of understanding you are looking for.

The children being assessed should be in your line of sight.

Teamwork – benefiting the children

When all of the adults work together as a team, it strengthens the message they want to give the children. It provides continuity for them in their learning. They can feel secure, being able to anticipate responses to their behaviour and emotional states. This in turn builds their self-esteem and their self-confidence as learners and as members of the community.

Continuity

'On Tuesday, I did adding-up sums with Mrs Hudson.'

'Yesterday, Mrs Hudson and I did more adding up but now, we had a hundreds column as well.'

'Today, the numbers in the hundreds column were bigger and we had to have the next column too.'

'When I work with Mrs Hudson, I just carry on from where I left off! She's nice and she explains things really well. I like Mrs Hudson!'

Tracy just carried on from where she left off. She didn't have to start again, cover old ground or try to work out how today's work fitted with the work she did yesterday. She was able to develop and improve. She increased her knowledge, improved her understanding, practised and developed her skills. Mrs Hudson enabled that progress. Mrs Hudson ensured continuity.

Continuity is a key ingredient in learning

Having continuity enables me to develop over time. Each thing I do is related to the things that I have done before. To achieve continuity, someone has to know how I learn and what happened last time.

● When I have continuity in my learning, my knowledge builds. It builds because each new fact is added to those I already know so that they are in a logical sequence with the new related to the old.

'Yesterday, we did an experiment and showed that light travels in a straight line. Today, we are going to see if that can help us to explain how a mirror works.'

● When I have continuity in my learning, my understanding grows. It grows because I can revisit and re-explore the ideas we discussed yesterday so that I focus on the areas I grasped least last time.

'We have already talked about the things that matter when you start a new settlement. So why did the Romans decide that London was important to them?'

● When I have continuity in my learning, my skills develop. They develop because I practise the particular elements that were not quite right last time.

'Last time we made dough, the bread didn't rise. We talked about it and realised that this was because there was not enough air in it. We know that air gets in when we knead the bread, so that is the skill we are going to practise.'

> **Top Tip**
>
> You can support continuity by a quick recap at the start of any activity which reminds children of previous relevant activities that they will develop. At the end, explain how you will develop their learning next time.
>
> **Put today in context. Say what came before and what is next.**

Security

Security state, feeling, means of being secure, a pledge, a surety, a guarantee…
(*Chambers 20th Century Dictionary*)

OK, so that's what the dictionary says. Your job is to deliver it. Unfortunately, it is not something you can parcel up and give to someone. It is not a certificate or even a reward. Security is about how I feel.

I feel secure because you are always there for me – you are kind and fair. You always do what you say you will do, even when it was not what I was hoping for. You never let me down and you always behave the same way. When you talk to me I feel that you are really interested in me – you care about me.

Children will expect you, as a professional, to be part of the system that gives them security. For some children, you may be the only thing in their life that they can rely on. For all children, you are a part of their world and they want to trust you.

You don't need to be anything other than yourself. Let the children get to know you. You are a nice person – let them see that you are. Just remember, the children are individuals and will want to be treated as such. Above all, be consistent in your attitude and the values you portray.

Top Tip

People who are being shouted at don't feel secure. They are more likely to feel that they are in a battle. You don't shout at people you know and like and get on with. How do you feel if someone shouts at you?

Use your normal voice, don't shout.

Planning with the class teacher

What I need and where I get it

If you are going to take one or more children for an activity, there are five things you must know.

1 The learning objective

This is the purpose of the activity. The activity has been set up to enable this. At the end of the session, this is what the child should have learned. Without learning objectives there is no lesson.

2 What

This covers what the child has to do, the resources available, where they are going to be, the order things have to be done, etc.

3 Outcome

The result of the activity. This is the evidence that the child will have left when they have finished. It only becomes evidence when you write on the back of the work.

4 How long

Your approach to the activity will vary depending on the time you are given to complete it.

5 Who

Do you get one child, a small group, the whole class? Will it be the same all the way through?

Take, for example, a lesson in a Year 1 class where the learning objective was to understand the terms 'greater than' and 'less than'. The teacher had given the assistant four children and a worksheet. The idea was for the assistant to throw a die four times and the children to put the numbers in the boxes of a sum laid out as follows.

Each child had a worksheet on which six of these sums were drawn. As the assistant threw the die, the numbers got filled in. George didn't understand at all.

The assistant realised this quite quickly and stopped the whole group. She asked the other three if they could explain to George what was going on. Sarah tried but she was the only one. The problem was that the four children did not really understand tens and units.

At this point the assistant produced a bag of money. She gave George 21p and Sarah 42p. The four children wrote down who had what and then had to decide who had the most money and why. She gave out different sums and kept asking them who had most and why. After 15 minutes, all four children had grasped the fact that they would have more if their number in the tens column was biggest.

The worksheet was never completed but all four children understood 'greater than' and 'less than'. All four had achieved the learning objective.

The teacher and the assistant had planned this session the previous Friday. The assistant was concerned that the four children might not understand. She had worked out the alternative approach and brought the bag of money along to help, just in case.

The most significant point is that the assistant knew in advance. In this illustration, the assistant knew well in advance the learning objective, the activity, the outcome, how long and who. This gave her the opportunity to think through the session and work out what to do if there were any difficulties.

> **Top Tip**
>
> The professional relationship is what matters. If you want to be friends as well, that's fine, but don't lose sight of where you are going. You need five things to be effective. Keep focused on those five.
>
> **Make sure you have the five key facts for every session.**

1. The five things I need were agreed in the weekly planning meeting I have with the teacher

2. The five things I need are in my copy of the teacher's planning

3. The five things I need are in the teacher's plans in their file

4. The five things I need are in the teacher's head

5. The five things have not been thought of yet

ask often enough there is a chance that the teacher will hand you a piece of paper. If they do, then you just skipped level 3 and are in level 2. They may even say 'OK, I've got a couple of minutes, let's talk about it.' Even better! Welcome to the Promised Land.

Assuming that you need to get to level 3 and you know the plans exist, try asking 'May I have a look at your plans for tomorrow at the end of school, please?' Keep asking each day, at the same time and in the same place and using the same words. The teacher might get fed up with you asking – so fed up that one day they turn round and say 'They're on my desk, please just look!' Level 3 achieved!

But don't stop at level 3. You now have permission to look. Now change the question. 'Do you mind if I take a copy of your plans for tomorrow at the end of school?' They will probably say go ahead, so take a copy. Now it is important to show how useful it is, so make sure it is clearly visible in each session. Don't forget to keep asking the same question every day, at the same time and in the same place and using the same words. One day the teacher might just turn around and give you a copy. Level 2 achieved!

And when you are given a copy of the plans, start asking simple questions. 'What does this mean?' 'How do I do that?' 'Where will I be able to find out more about this?' 'What shall I try if George doesn't understand?'

A road to the Promised Land

Every time you work with children, you need to know five things. Where are they?

For every teacher you work with and in each session you do, the five things you need will be in one of the categories above. The top is the Promised Land and should be where we all are. Before you laugh, there are some who will read this and know that they are already there. For the rest, we need to find the path to get there.

I'm going to assume that the teacher you work with is competent. This means that stages 4 and 5 don't exist. If you have a teacher who is at 5 you need to start asking questions such as, 'Any thoughts about what we might be doing in literacy tomorrow?' This should move them up to level 4.

If you suspect that they are at level 4, try, 'Mind if I jot down your ideas for literacy tomorrow?' If you

What is a meeting?

An American businessman gave a lecture on the art of workplace communication. He said that he had a simple definition of a meeting. He said, 'You put two or more people in the same place at the same time, and get three questions asked and answered, that's a meeting!' He also said, 'Never ask for a meeting, no one has the time. Just get them to answer three of your questions. I won't tell them it's a meeting if you don't!'

Armed with your copy of the plan, ask questions. Start with one and build up to three. That's a meeting. It's also the Promised Land.

Eventually the meetings will be programmed in. In one school, teachers meet with their assistants for an hour on a Friday afternoon while the headteacher takes a school assembly. In another, each teacher has a weekly planning session with their assistants while a specialist teacher takes their class for music. A third school pays the assistants to attend a Wednesday evening planning session each week.

There are many solutions to the problem but they only become a solution when each school recognises it has a problem. If your school doesn't have a solution yet, then they may need some help to realise they have a problem. They may not know it is a problem unless you tell them. After all, don't you feel so much better when you know what you are doing? And isn't it so much better when you know in advance?

Planning meetings

Once you have reached the Promised Land it is important to make the most of it. This means that you need to get as much as you can from the meeting. This means that you have to be well prepared and focused.

Before the meeting starts, work out all the sessions in which you will take part. For each of these prepare a sheet ready to fill in the five key facts. Now you are ready for the meeting.

At the meeting, you must focus on getting the gaps in your sheets filled in. Let the meeting flow, and fill in as you go along. Before the meeting ends, go back over the gaps and ask specific

> **Top Tip**
>
> I can argue with you when you tell me what you think. I can disagree with you and I can tell you that you are wrong. I can even pull rank. You will end up feeling put down. However, if you tell me how you feel, I can't ignore you, you are not wrong and I can't pull rank. You will have made your point just as effectively and you won't end up feeling put down.
>
> **Tell me how you feel and not what you think.**

questions to fill the gaps. 'In science on Tuesday, you want me to do the experiment with four children – which four?' 'You said that we would do the worksheet in literacy – how long will we have?' By the end of the meeting you should have all your gaps filled.

If your teacher is well organised, they will bring planning sheets to the meeting as a basis for discussion. If you know this is going to happen then you won't need to prepare your own sheets. However, it is still worth making sure that you have paper and pen for the other notes you may want to make.

The teacher's planning sheets should be really helpful. They should contain your five things. Try taking a highlighter pen with you so that you can mark all the parts that are important to you. It makes finding them easier later on.

At the meeting, make sure you understand the learning objective. Be very clear what the teacher wants the children to know, understand or be able to do as a result of the activity. When you are clear about this, consider how you will record each child's achievement. Discuss this with the teacher and try to devise a record that does not use words.

You also need to discuss the activity itself. If it is particularly complicated or you are not sure how it works, try to put a few minutes aside before the session so that you can have a go yourself. It is really important to ensure that what you get the children to do will actually deliver the learning objective. It is also important to make sure that you know where the children are going so that you are not discovering with them at the same time.

Finally, remember to share any thoughts you have that may make the learning opportunities better. It may be that you have noticed that George works better when he has something in his hands or that Sarah seems to understand things better when she gets them as a picture. Slight alterations to the way something is done can make all the difference to how well particular children learn.

Top Tip

Take your plans to the lesson in a folder or ring file but slip each plan into a plastic sleeve first. It prevents your plans being destroyed when they get liquid accidentally poured over them. Each day you can take that day's plans out of the plastic sleeves and put in those for the next day. Try and make your file distinctive. Make it a different colour or cover it with something that stands out. Show your file to the children. Make sure they know it is yours – then, when you can't find it, everyone knows what they are looking for.

Be prepared for the unexpected.

The inspectors are calling

What to expect

The inspectors are interested in finding out how well the children are getting on. The starting point is to look at the children's performance in relation to children in other schools. To do this they will look at the percentage of children achieving Level 2 at age 7, and Level 4 at age 11. There are national benchmarks for each of these and your school's performance will be compared with these.

From this, inspectors will form an opinion and they will then seek to identify the factors that influence the performance of your school. Critically, they will try to find out what the school thinks of itself. This is called school self-evaluation.

The inspectors will examine the self-evaluation to find out whether it is accurate and whether it leads to a plan to either improve or maintain the standards being achieved.

If the school is found to have an accurate picture of itself and a clear and effective plan for the future, then the outcome of the inspection will be positive.

What you should expect is that inspectors will visit your sessions either to validate the standards that the school thinks it has or to evaluate the accuracy of the self-evaluation and the subsequent action plan.

> ### Top Tip
>
> Inspectors do not have to see you at work. There is no guarantee that you will be seen or spoken to. If you want to be seen by an inspector, then ask an inspector to come to a particular session. You still may not get a visit, but they will try to come.
>
> **If you want a visit, ask for one.**

Being observed

Inspectors don't always announce where they are going in advance. This isn't because they want to catch you out, but it gives them more flexibility to go where they want and to respond to what is happening. It is possible that the first you will know of the visit is when the door opens and the inspector slides in. They may even be standing outside the room waiting for you and the children to arrive.

If appropriate, the inspector will introduce himself or herself but, if you are busy or the lesson is under way, then they will not interrupt. They will glance around the room and identify a place where they can sit or hover without getting in the way. While doing this they will also be looking for some indication of what is happening or is about to happen in the session. This is your first opportunity to help.

In some lessons there is the inspector's chair with a lesson plan waiting. This will be useful but don't expect your inspector to stay where you put them for long. Don't underestimate the value of telling them what is happening. In particular, make sure they know how many children should be in the lesson and how many have which sort of special need. They will also need to know the learning objectives and what the children will do.

During the lesson, either they will review the whole group or they will focus on a particular aspect. For example, they may be interested in whether the girls do as well as the boys or whether children of Afro-Caribbean ethnicity do as well as those from

a European background. Whatever the focus, the first job will be to determine the levels the children are achieving.

They will try to identify what the children actually understand, know and can do and they will use this to justify a National Curriculum level for each level of ability in the group. These ability levels are then compared with the national expectations to see whether they are below, at, or above them.

The second judgement the inspector will try to make is about the level of achievement. This is different from the attainment level. **Attainment** is measured against a national figure whereas **achievement** is a measurement of how well children are doing in relation to their own ability.

The third and fourth judgements are about teaching and learning. These two are inextricably linked. If learning is poor then teaching cannot be even satisfactory, and excellent teaching automatically promotes learning of the highest level.

The final judgements are about children's behaviour and attitude. Poorly behaved children don't learn and it is not just the behaviour that will be scrutinised but also how you react to or promote patterns of behaviour.

In all the judgements the inspector will try to interact with the children and may well discuss current and previous work with them. You don't need to create a space for this to happen. Nor should you change your process of delivery to accommodate them. You are in charge and the inspector will fit in around you.

In discussion

Inspectors have to talk to people who affect the judgements they make. Different types of inspection make different judgements. A starting point for inspections is always what a school thinks of itself and what it was asked to consider at the time of the last inspection. Inspectors try to see if the school's view of itself is accurate and whether the issues that were raised previously have now been addressed.

In gathering their evidence, inspectors will try to interview those staff who are able to contribute valuable facts or insights. You may be one of them. If you are, the inspector will try to arrange a mutually convenient time to talk to you. You shouldn't feel threatened by this and you don't have to be on your own. In many cases, inspectors will talk to representatives of the team of assistants or even all of them at once. Sometimes they will want to talk to just you. Even in this situation, you can take someone with you.

If an inspector does want to talk to you, it will be because you are responsible for something. The discussion will focus on what you do and how you do it. The inspector is not trying to catch you out. He or she is only interested in gathering evidence to show how well the school supports its children.

Suppose, for example, you are responsible for the delivery of additional literacy support (ALS). The questions are likely to cover the following topics.

1   How do you know how well children are doing?

2   How do you know what they had attained when they started?

3   How do you decide what they will do next?

4   Who do you go to if you are not sure about something?

5   How are the children selected to work with you?

6   What happens if you need some resources that you don't have?

7   Have you had the opportunity to participate in any training recently?

8   Does anyone ever come and watch you at work and then give you feedback?

9   What meetings are you invited to regularly or occasionally?

This is not a definitive list but it does give a few ideas of typical questions. Each question has a particular purpose. You may want to show the inspector your records (question 1) or your planning (question 3). There may be baseline assessments (question 2) and selection criteria (question 5).

If the inspector asks for something that you don't have to hand, then tell him or her that you have it and will make it available at a specified time and place. If you don't know the answer to a question, then say so.

Just remember that inspection is a two-way process. The inspectors will want to paint a fair picture of the school and they can only do that if the school shares everything with them. If you have something that you think is important and useful, don't wait to be asked for it – volunteer it!

Getting feedback

If an inspector does see you in action, they will not necessarily offer you feedback. They must, however, give you feedback if you ask for it.

The feedback will focus on two themes. Firstly, the inspector will identify the strengths of the session seen. This means that he or she will go through what worked well and why it worked. Secondly, the inspector will identify anything that he or she considers to be something that could have worked better. These are the areas for improvement.

It is important for you to hear the balance of what is said. It is very easy to come away remembering one small criticism in an ocean of positive statements. Try to remember the overall balance.

It is also important to remember that the inspector is not passing an overall judgement on you. These are merely observations about what did or didn't work in the short period of time that the inspector was with you. Only you can put these comments in the context of your work. Was this a typical session? Are the comments justified? Did you act in the same way as usual or differently?

The purpose of the feedback is to encourage you to think about what you do. If you think about what is said, then the process is worthwhile.

> **Top Tip**
>
> If you are given feedback, keep it in proportion. You know how typical it is of what you normally do. If there is criticism, there may be a good reason for it. The inspector has no reason to tell anything other than their opinion of what they saw.
>
> **Feedback from an inspector is independent and this makes it valuable.**

Responding to children

When you work with children, you establish a relationship. The relationship is based on body language and communication. You need to consider key aspects of these when you work with and respond to children.

Questions and answers

We use a lot of questions when working with children. It is sometimes interesting to see how many. Here is a game you can try to see the impact of questions. Set yourself a task to explain one thing to two children, one at a time. When you work with the first child you may not use any questions at all. When you work with the second, you can use only questions.

The first style is similar to that used by lecturers. They broadcast information and make no attempt to identify whether anyone understands anything during the lecture. The second style is one of coaching. You never tell the person anything.

You get them to understand by responding to a continuous stream of questions.

You are likely to find both styles difficult and uncomfortable. Neither is used continuously in teaching. Both, however, are valuable techniques and both highlight the fact that the question is not a simple tool but is quite complex.

Questions are of many different types. We will try a simple model for classifying questions and then see how they fit. We can start by dividing questions into two main groups – closed questions and open questions.

Closed questions

Closed questions have a single answer – 'What is the capital of England?', 'What is 22 add 47?'.

Open questions

Open questions have more than one possible answer – 'What is your favourite book?', 'Can you tell me something about the Romans?'.

CLOSED	Broadcast	Machine-gun	Pointed	Rhetoric	Loaded	Leading	Win–win	Can't fail	Yes/No
Discipline									
Prompting			A						
Involving									
Reflective								C	
Assessment					D				
Counselling									
Summary									
Process						B			
Fishing									

OPEN	Broadcast	Machine-gun	Pointed	Rhetoric	Loaded	Leading	Win–win	Can't fail	Yes/No
Discipline									
Prompting									
Involving	Y						X		
Reflective									
Assessment		W							
Counselling									
Summary			Z						
Process									
Fishing									

We will now add two more dimensions. We will consider why the question was asked and how the question was asked. These are also referred to as the **motivation** and the **style**. We can now draw a pair of question classification grids (see p37).

Every question is either open or closed and has a recognised style and a motivation for asking it. To illustrate the point, here are eight examples using the letters in the grid.

A 'Come on then George, can you think hard about what an adverb is?' It is rhetoric because you don't expect an answer. It is prompting because it encourages George to think. It is closed because there is only one answer.

B 'So did you add the three to the two next or the two to the three?' It is a can't fail question because, whichever the child says, they are correct. It is a process question because it is asking the child to take you through the next stage of the process, and it is closed because there is only one answer in reality.

C 'Think back, did the gear wheel go on next?' It is yes/no because these are the only two possible answers, it is reflective because it asks the children to think back to a previous event, and it is closed because there is only one correct answer.

D 'Was this when you decided to hold down the Shift key?' This is leading because it is asking the child to agree with the suggestion in the question. It is assessment because it is seeking to discover if they know. It is closed because it has only one answer.

W 'Sarah, can you name a colour?' 'George, can you name a colour?' 'Karen, can you name a colour?' It is machine-gun because the same question is repeated in quick succession. It is assessment because it is trying to see who knows something, and it is open because there is more than one answer.

X 'George, would you like to choose a new book first, or would you like to suggest the title for our next story?' It is win–win because you don't mind which the child opts for. It is involving because it draws the child into an activity, and it is open because there is more than one answer.

Y 'Who wants to tell me about their best friend?' It is broadcast because the question applies to everyone, it is involving because everyone can answer the question, and it is open because there is more than one answer.

Z 'Sarah, can you tell me what happened next?' This is pointed because it is Sarah who has been asked. It is summary because the child is invited to describe part of a sequence, and it is open because there is more than one answer.

Have a go at writing questions that fit into the gaps on the grid. This exercise has two main points. Firstly, it encourages you to explore the range of questions that you could be using. Secondly, it is a way of identifying different teaching styles.

Make a copy of the two grids and take them to a lesson (it's probably a good idea to chat to the teacher about what you want to do). In the lesson, listen to the questions the teacher asks and put ticks in the boxes on the grids. Have a chat to the teacher about what the pattern should look like and whether the pattern would change in different types of lesson. Does the pattern give you any clues about involving children or the quality of learning taking place?

Being in charge

Children have to be clear about who is in charge. When they are working with you, you are! This isn't about discipline, it is just about getting the message across. You can do this effectively in fairly subtle ways. Here are a few tips that should help.

Eye level

If you are working with more than one child, make sure your eye level is significantly higher than theirs. This means that, if they are sitting on the floor, you can sit on a chair. If they are sitting in their chairs, stand up.

Position

Take up a position where you know that every child you are working with can see you. You should be in their line of sight. They should not have to move even their head for a clear view. You can arrange this by moving the furniture before the children arrive. It's a good idea not to stand with your back to the window because the children will see you in silhouette and may be distracted by the bright light in their eyes.

Stillness

Nervous people jig about a lot. Practise a standing position which is comfortable and which you can maintain for some time without moving about. When the children are watching you, you should exude confidence. You won't look confident if you are moving about. Movement should be purposeful.

Fix

All sessions should start the same way – everyone silent and all eyes on you. Wait for it. It doesn't matter how long you have to wait, just wait. While you are waiting, say nothing and keep your face expressionless. If it is going on a bit, make sure they see you looking at your watch, otherwise find two points on the wall opposite, about ten feet apart, and stare at them alternately. You can, occasionally say things like, 'I'm not starting until everyone is silent and looking at me.' Or, 'I'm still waiting.' Don't raise your voice and don't shout over the noise. When you get what you are waiting for, remember to say thank you. Whatever you do, don't start until you have 100 per cent attention.

Maintain

If, at any point, you lose the 100 per cent attention, stop. Even if you are in mid-sentence, just stop. Now wait for full attention again.

Language

We all respond well to positive language. It draws us in and makes us feel wanted. Negative language has the opposite effect. Try to abide by two simple rules when working with a child.

1 Never tell a child they are wrong.

2 Teaching is dialogue.

1 Never tell a child they are wrong

The temptation is sometimes huge and there are times we do it without thinking. However, there is always an alternative. Consider this example.

'George, what is 2+2?'

'5'

At this point it is almost a reflex reaction to say 'no'. But, there are alternatives.

'OK, George, tell me how you worked it out.' (I'm holding up two fingers on my left hand and two fingers on my right hand.) 'How many fingers am I holding up on this hand George? … Now, how many on my other hand? … Will you count them all for me?'

'Would you like to think again, George?'

'Have another go, George.'

'Sarah, do you agree with George? … Perhaps you can tell George how you worked it out.'

The fact that George doesn't know is not his failure, but your opportunity. It is your chance to reinforce the process – it is your chance to involve the other children in an explanation. It is your chance to get George to try again.

It also makes sure that George feels good about what he is doing. Instead of being told he is wrong, he is getting support and encouragement.

2 Teaching is a dialogue

It takes more than one person, and everyone involved needs to understand the words. It is really important to make sure that everyone is included all of the time.

Giving instructions

There is a real art to giving instructions. To start with, don't ask a child to do two things until they have proved they can do one.

'Get your books out, open them at the last piece of work and draw a line across the page. Put today's date and the title "Judaism". Don't forget to underline them both.'

That is seven instructions in one. Now, some children will manage this quite easily, more because it is a routine than anything else. Others will struggle. Until you know that the children you are working with can manage more than one thing at a time, give them just one instruction at a time.

There is a process that works really well. You know when you have done it properly because no one asks what they have to do two seconds after you say 'go'. If you use the following five-step system it should ensure a smooth start to the activity.

Step 1 – Tell the children what they have to do

Break it down into simple steps. Articulate each clearly and precisely. Make sure the steps are in the correct order. Emphasise the order and any health and safety points.

'You will each need one worksheet and four different colour pencils.
A triangle is a shape with three sides.
You have to find a triangle on the sheet and colour it in.
You now look for another triangle and colour that in, using a different colour.
Now find two more and colour them in in different colours.
When you have finished, you will have coloured in four triangles, each in a different colour.
You will have five minutes to finish.'

Step 2 – Get two or three children to repeat to the group what has to be done

Listen carefully and make sure they give each step in the correct order. Emphasise the key points as they say them and make any corrections or additions necessary. Make sure any points on health and safety are repeated each time.

'Sarah, can you tell us all what we have to do?'
'Tell me again, how many colour pencils do we each need?'
'Thank you. Now, George, can you tell us all what we have to do?'
'Just remind me how many sides a triangle has.'
'Thank you.'

Step 3 – Any questions?

Invite the children to ask any questions at all. Some of the questions will be about the task. Deal with these by reinforcing the steps in what has to be done. Some of the questions will have nothing to do with the task at all. These must also be dealt with positively. Instead of telling the child that the question is not relevant, tell them when the question will be dealt with. If you don't do this, you run the risk that the child will be so diverted by not having an answer that they don't concentrate on the lesson.

'Any questions?'
'Yes George, any four triangles on the sheet.'
'If the triangles overlap, Sarah, then the bit that is part of both triangles will have to be coloured with both pencils.'
'There are lots of triangles on the sheet, George, you just have to find them. You won't need to draw any of your own.'

'Thank you, George, you can tell us all about your trip last Sunday just before we go for lunch.'
'Try and do all four in the five minutes.'
'Yes, Sarah, yellow and blue are a lovely combination but everyone can use any four different colours.'

Keep asking if there are any questions until none are forthcoming.

'Any more questions?'
'OK!'

Step 4 – Tell the children what they have to do again

As before, break it down into simple steps. Articulate each clearly and precisely. Make sure the steps are in the correct order. Emphasise the order and any health and safety points.

This is an important step because, after the question session, some children will have forgotten what to do.

'You need one worksheet and four colour pencils, all different.
Remember, a triangle has three sides.
Find a triangle. Colour it in.
Find another. Colour it in a different colour.
Find two more. Colour them in different colours.
You finish with four coloured triangles.
You have five minutes.'

Step 5 – Say 'Go!'

You will know if you have succeeded by the number of children who need help to get going. If there are lots of children needing help straight away, then you either included too many steps or gave a poor explanation. In this situation, don't battle against a sea of questions. Stop everyone and start all over again. This time use the five-step approach but break the whole thing into separate parts and deal with one at a time.

When you structure the start of an activity like this, it means that everyone has a good chance of getting it right.

Don't stand back at this stage. Find someone who is doing it right. When you have found them, stop everyone for a moment.

'George, that is brilliant! Hold it up! I want everyone to look at the triangle that George has coloured blue. Well done, George! Carry on, everyone.'

By stopping everyone, you are able to reinforce what success looks like. All the children will now be reassured by seeing what George has achieved. In addition, George is going to feel pretty good about what he is doing. He will be very motivated to continue his work. If you choose your 'George' carefully, you can control his behaviour with positive reinforcement.

Managing children

Managing children is different when you work with a whole class from when you work with a small group or one-to-one.

Whole class

The important thing with a whole class is to establish who is in charge. The key points for this have already been covered but it is important to emphasise that this matters.

It is also worth making sure that when you want everyone to stop and pay attention, it happens. Use the same routine and be consistent. Teachers use lots of different ways to achieve this.

- There is the teacher who starts counting, sometimes up and sometimes down. The children know that they have to be silent and listening when the teacher gets to a particular number.

- Then there is the teacher who puts her hands on her head. Any child who sees this does the same until everyone is quiet, listening and with their hands on their head.

- One teacher has a little bell. She rings it when she wants the class to stop and listen.

- In another class the teacher merely says, 'Will you all pay attention to me please?' He gets an instant deafening silence.

The point is that each of these is a routine. It is also consistent. The children know what it is and what they are expected to do. That is why it works every time.

Top Tip

When you work with a large group for the first time, tell them what you will do when you want their attention. Now show them what it looks like and have a practice. You can even make a game out of it. The purpose is to make sure that, when you use it for real, no child is able to say truthfully that they didn't know what you meant.

Work out a system for getting attention and teach it to the class.

Groups

Don't sit down. You are not a member of the group, so stand up. When you stand up, you tell the group that you are in charge. Standing makes your eye level higher – a key factor in taking control in groups.

If you stand up, the children will wait for your lead. That is where you take charge and start the five-step introduction to the task (see 'Giving instructions' on p39).

The learning objective is the most important part of the activity. You have to know who understands the learning objective and who doesn't. If everyone seems to be working, stop the group and get several to explain what they are doing. Now you will know. Of course, if one child clearly hasn't got a clue, get the others to explain it to him. Then he gets more explanations and you find out who really understood.

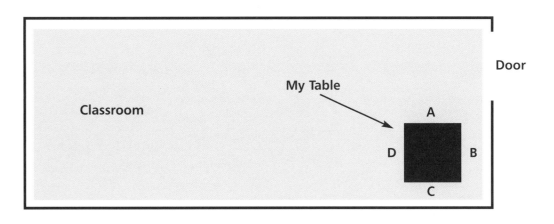

Your position is important. Consider the classroom layout on p41. It shows the wall, the door and the table you will be working at. You are not going to sit down but you will have to decide which side of the table to work from. The sides are labelled A, B, C and D. Which side would you choose in this classroom?

It is possible to come up with a good reason for any side but, in this classroom, there is only one place for most – C. C is unique in this room. It is the only place you can stand that has the door in your line of sight. Nothing will get in or out of the room without you knowing. It will have to pass right in front of your eyes.

Now you won't get caught out when the headteacher 'borrows' your teacher for a minute. And, as for George, he won't be sliding off without you knowing. For you, in this room, the only place to be is at C – you're going to do everything from C. You can see everything from there, including the teacher and the rest of the class.

Now you know you are going to stand at C, look at the wall directly in front of you. If there isn't a clock there, get one and put it there. You need to know what the time is so that you know how long you have left. You could keep looking at your watch but that is distracting. You need the clock in your line of sight. You'll know the time but they won't know that you're looking.

> **Top Tip**
>
> Always assume that the task you have been asked to complete with the group will last for less time than you have been given.
>
> **Have 'Plan B' ready!** (See p60.)

One-to-one

In a one-to-one situation, left-handed children should sit on your left. Right-handed children should sit on your right. Keep a record in your mark book of which hand each child writes with so that you can direct them to the correct seat from the start.

When you sit, you should face each other across the corner of a table. It gives you close proximity, you can see their work and you have eye contact.

One-to-one is very difficult to do well. It is probably happening because the child has a particular problem. This may be a curriculum problem, which means they come to you for focused curriculum work, or it may be because they have a special need. What you have to do is provide the additional support without creating dependence.

Eventually the child may have to survive without one-to-one support so it is important that your actions do not make them dependent on it. Part of your task is to give them the confidence to work without the extra support.

> **Top Tip**
>
> Make sure that you are well prepared. Have everything to hand and make the best use of the time available. There should always be some reinforcement, some revision and something new. The balance may change but all three elements should be there.
>
> **Prepare thoroughly.**

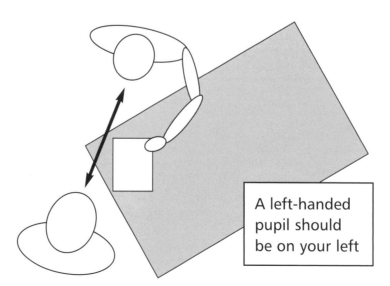

A left-handed pupil should be on your left

Managing behaviour

Successful behaviour management is about not appearing to manage behaviour at all. If you watch the best teachers at work, you will soon realise that discipline is not an issue and the children just seem to do what they are asked.

Achieving this is not easy but there are a number of simple steps that you can take towards achieving this goal. However, the most important thing to have is confidence. All the best teachers ooze confidence. Their ability to handle the class is never in question and they always seem to know what to do in every situation.

You must remember that all behaviour is learned and that changing a pattern of behaviour can take a very long time. This means that it is really important to establish the pattern from the start.

The behaviour pattern you promote is one that children should adopt any time they are with you. Their behaviour will change depending on whom they are with. This is true for all of us. You behave differently with a colleague, a friend and a casual acquaintance. The same is true for the children. This means that you are not looking for them to treat you the same as someone else – rather you are looking for them to follow your pattern.

Ultimately, you will have to develop your own style. You will have to win the trust and belief of each child. What follows are a few ideas that will help you along the way.

Establishing the ground rules

1 Make sure everyone knows what you believe in and what you stand for

It is very easy to assume that the children know what to expect – but they won't unless you tell them. Make it clear to them what is acceptable to you and what is not. When you give positive feedback to children who are doing things right, it serves as a reminder to everyone of the behaviour you expect.

> 'John, you are sitting very nicely, thank you.'
> 'Sarah, thank you for not interrupting. I know you were dying to say something and now it's your turn.'

2 Show children where the line is drawn

Children don't always know what is acceptable and what is not. If you don't tell them what they can

and can't do, they will 'try you out'. This is not being naughty, it is merely an attempt to identify your boundaries. You make things easier for everyone when you show the children where the line is drawn.

> 'We all like to have fun, but when I say that it's time to work, we need to settle down quickly.'

3 Be consistent in the standards you expect

If it was acceptable yesterday, then it is acceptable today. If it wasn't allowed yesterday, then it shouldn't be allowed today. Even more important, if one child can do something, then they all can, and if one child is not allowed, then none should be.

There was a class where there was one child with very disturbed behaviour. Unfortunately, when he was good, he was rewarded with sweets. The rest of the class really resented this. After all, they were good all the time – so they should have lots of sweets! The problem is that the rules were different and this doesn't work.

The other problem with using rewards is that the child will end up doing something to get the reward. What we want to happen is that the child behaves because they feel good about it.

> **Top Tip**
>
> Make the reward simple and the same for everyone. Any time someone gets it right, it is a mark of respect for you. Always acknowledge it.
>
> **Just say 'Thank you'.**

Avoiding conflict

Direct instructions and blunt enquiries are the language of conflict. Try to avoid conflict statements and questions. Consider this example.

> 'Where are you going?'

This is short and blunt. It can easily be replaced by a question that encourages a dialogue.

> 'Hello George, you look very cheerful, are you off on an errand somewhere?'

Try rewording some of these so that each is positive and encourages a dialogue instead of being aggressive.

> 'What did you do that for?'
> 'Don't call out!'
> 'Sit down and don't move until I tell you to!'

Sarcasm should also be avoided because it can easily be misunderstood. When George trips and falls, you should avoid saying

> 'Well done, George, very good!'

Try to be a little more understanding and straightforward instead.

> 'Oh dear! Are you all right, George?'

Top Tip

Before you make a short, sharp statement, stop and think about what you are about to say. Can you say it in a different way? Can you take the challenge out so that the child does not feel as if you are attacking them?

When you think positively, you speak positively.

Deflecting aggression

If someone is being aggressive towards you, it is important to remember that it probably isn't personal, you just happen to be a convenient target. It always takes two to have an argument, so don't be drawn. If the argument starts, both of you will want to win and that escalates the problem. Instead, try to take the heat out of the situation. Be measured in your response. Ask questions instead of making statements. Talk calmly and quietly. Make eye contact but don't stare. Keep your arms still, don't wave them about. In other words, make sure you behave in the exact opposite way to the aggressor.

Sometimes you will be able to respond by empathising with the statement. This puts you on their side rather than against them. As an example, the aggressor might say

> 'He just pushed in! He can't do that!'

This gives you the chance to empathise with how he feels.

> 'I know just how you feel. I get really wound up when I've been standing in a queue for ages and then someone pushes in.'

Defuse the situation by showing a way out.

> 'Last time I felt like that, I took a deep breath and counted to ten, then I felt better.'

Manage by manipulation

It is amazing how much of our behaviour is manipulated and how accepting we are. Most of us cross the road on a crossing when we can see one. Few of us would think of moving a table and chair in a restaurant – we sit where we are put even when it is in a draught or by a door. In Britain, most of us join the back of a queue – that's not the case in some other cultures!

It is also amazing how easily we follow a lead. Walk down the street one day and then stop and look up at the top of a building. Fix your gaze on a point and just stare. It's almost irresistible. Nearly everyone will look up to see what you are looking at. Some might even stand next to you. If you get a big enough crowd you can even walk away and leave them to it!

What this means is that you can exploit these very human traits to manage children's behaviour in a positive way.

Every time you settle somewhere to work, mark your place with a place marker. Your place marker is the thing that you carry around everywhere. It may be a file, a glasses case, a bag, a book, anything in fact. The key is that everyone knows it is yours.

Adults tend not to move someone else's place marker. Even when you don't know whose it is, you still won't touch it. We put coats on seats and towels on sunbeds to 'reserve' our place.

Children will also leave a place marker alone, but only if they know whose it is. So you need to introduce your place marker to the children so that they know it is yours. Now, when you put it in the place you want to work, most children will not only leave it alone, they will go somewhere else because they will recognise that you have booked that place.

You can even have place markers for the children. A simple name tag works and in some classes the tables are associated with colours or shapes. These are non-verbal ways of directing children to where they should be.

Another sure way of getting children to sit in the pattern you want is to put the chairs in the pattern before the children arrive. Similarly, if you remove a chair from a place where you don't want anyone to sit, the chance of a child sitting there is much smaller since they would have to carry a chair to that place first.

If you are working with a group and one child is not fully involved, you could tell them off. However, a much better way of dealing with them is to make them your next volunteer. It draws them back into the activity and involves them in what is happening.

> **Top Tip**
>
> Small children get led by their hands. Occupy the hands and you occupy their minds. In one lesson the teacher wanted to do counting. The first task was to hold up two hands and wiggle the fingers. Not only could they all do it, it also kept every hand occupied and out of trouble.
>
> **Make sure very young children know what to do with their hands.**

Separating the person from the behaviour

When you are dealing with issues of behaviour, it is essential that the child knows that it is their behaviour that you did not like – they themselves are OK. You must separate the two and make the distinction obvious.

> 'George, you are a really nice lad but when you kick someone you make me feel really sad. Do you want me to feel sad?'

This separates George, who is a really nice boy, from the behaviour, which is kicking people. Not only that, I haven't told George that he is wrong, I have told him how it makes me feel. I can then ask him if he wants to make me feel like that. When he says he doesn't, he will realise that I won't feel sad when he stops kicking. I achieve the same end but I can do it positively.

Respond with your feelings

You should always tell children how you feel about what they do. It is very powerful both as a reward and as an incentive. You should use it equally for nice feelings and sad feelings. If you do, you will find that you are praising far more than you are correcting.

We often neglect to praise. It is something we should do more often.

> 'George, you have just finished four sentences in five minutes without me having to say anything at all. You have worked really well. That is great. Now I feel really good about that. Thank you.'

The first time you do this, George is going to be a bit surprised because he isn't used to it. After a while he will share the warm glow you are describing and enjoy it.

Note how what you say contains the key ingredients of praise.

- Who are you praising? George.
- What did they do right? Four sentences, five minutes, no prompts.
- What was your reaction? Great!
- How did you feel? Really good.
- What was the reward? 'Thank you'.

You use exactly the same structure when you need to correct the way the child behaves.

'George, you have now been sitting there for five minutes and, as yet, you have written nothing. I am very disappointed. I feel really sad. Please try again.'

- Who are you addressing? George.

- What is the problem? Five minutes, no sentences.

- What was your reaction? Very disappointed.

- How did you feel? Really sad.

- What was the reward? 'Please try again.'

Neither of these responses invites a discussion. Both are straight statements. In neither case can the child argue with what is said. You told the child what they did or did not do, which should be a fact, and you told the child how you felt, which is not something they would know.

Some people do get into a debate with the child. When this happens there is a danger that the focus will move away from the incident into a broader arena. In the instances shown, the effect is short and sharp. It is also important that the positive and negative are, at the very least, balanced. By preference there will be more that is positive than negative. It is always possible to find something positive to respond to.

Catch them doing it right

This is a mindset. Too often we only notice children when they do something wrong. It doesn't take them long to realise that if they do something wrong they get noticed. Getting noticed means getting attention. Attention is exactly what some children crave. Hence they misbehave to get it.

Suppose, however, that you made a point of catching children getting it right! It won't take them long to realise that when they get it right they get noticed. They now have to get it right in order to get attention.

Suddenly, you have entered the positive mindset. You will no longer see a sequence of disjointed errors but a flowing tide of super achievements. Your whole attitude will change. Your approach will change. The children will see you differently and they will behave differently.

A school trip to a London theatre involved a train journey. The children were of secondary age and very streetwise. The teacher waited with them on the platform and, when the train arrived, everyone got on. There were children in practically every carriage and this train had no corridor. Two stops later we all got off. The teacher counted heads and we set off for the theatre.

Some time later the teacher was asked whether she had been worried about how the children would behave on the train, whether they would upset the other passengers and whether they might try a quiet puff in the corner. She just smiled and said, 'If I expect the worst, I usually get the worst. When I expect the best, I usually get the best. I feel happy with the best and I like feeling happy.'

Of course you don't always need to say something. There are other ways to reward the child who is doing it right. In the above example, the children got the chance for a second theatre trip. Sometimes you just need a nod or a wink. A touch on an elbow with a whispered 'Nice one!' can be as effective as a simple smile or thumbs-up.

The point is that you have moved on. You now think positively.

For more information on promoting positive behaviour and catching the children being good, see *The Positive Behaviour Handbook*, also from pfp publishing.

Angry children

We all have an outburst sometimes. It is part of human nature. Children are human so they will have an outburst occasionally. The outburst has been likened to a safety valve. Without it you would blow up. Sometimes the outburst is a fit of temper, sometimes it goes further and becomes aggressive as well.

As adults we devise ways of dealing with the slow build-up of tension. Often we can see it coming. Some people deal with it by getting involved in a sport, perhaps hitting squash balls. Some people deal with it through working out, walking, running, cycling, etc.

Most adults can see it coming but we can all still lose our temper. Children are no different in the way the tension builds, but they don't always have a strategy for dealing with it. Give them space to cool down. When they are calm, talk to them about when they knew it was becoming a problem and what they could do next time.

There is also another type of anger that some children face. The anger arises because the child is faced with a conflict they cannot resolve. An example of this is the child who gets confused because the behaviour they exhibit in one setting is deemed acceptable yet the same behaviour in another setting is not.

It is likely that this child is bringing behaviour that is normal outside school into school and is being told that it is unacceptable. In this situation, it is

not sufficient to tell the child that their behaviour in school is wrong. The focus should be on teaching the child what normal behaviour inside school means.

You are never going to change the world but you can teach a child what constitutes acceptable behaviour in school. It is a positive approach that gives the child an alternative. It is not the negative approach that tells the child what they can't do and then leaves a vacuum with nothing to fill it.

Children who need this support are likely to show one of two characteristics.

- They may appear to have very little reaction in a difficult situation. For example, they don't notice someone getting very upset or seem untouched by the fight in the playground. The reaction they show seems unusual because it is very accepting of behaviour that is far from the normal.

- Alternatively, the child may appear to have an angry reaction to fairly trivial situations and they repeat these actions often enough for others to start worrying about them.

These children need the support of a programme that teaches them how to behave in the context of the school. Your school will use such a programme if needed.

Worried children

Most of us worry at some time and children are no different. Worry arises because you haven't yet sorted out how to deal with a situation. When you know how to deal with it, you worry less.

Some people worry more than others. Some worry about things that others don't worry about. Few of us worry whether the sun will rise tomorrow and

To help a child it is first necessary to spot that they are worrying. The telltale signs are sudden changes in behaviour or in performance. Look for the child who suddenly does less work, at a lower standard than usual, or whose work suddenly gets untidy, or whose work is unfinished. Look for the child who goes very quiet or suddenly becomes aggressive. The change can be caused by many things but if you have noticed the change, make sure the teacher has as well.

The child may find it helpful to talk about the thing that worries them or they may not. You can be available to them but it is their decision. If they don't want to talk to you, don't make them. Just make sure you have shared your concern for them.

Sick children

There are children taken ill at school and children who come to school when they are ill. Sometimes children start to feel ill on the way.

Your school will have a procedure for dealing with children who are ill and you should know what it is. In many schools the procedure will be to provide somewhere quiet for the child to sit or lie and many schools will contact the parent or carer so that the child can be collected.

If you are with an ill child, give them space and check on them regularly. If they want to chat then do, but let the child take the lead.

Some children take medication. You cannot be required to give any child any sort of medicine. Some schools insist a parent or carer comes to the school to give a drug if it is needed. If you choose to give a drug to a child, you do so as a volunteer and not as a member of staff.

what we'll do if it doesn't. Nearly all of us will have worried about some or all of these – money, being late, what someone might think of us, what might turn up in the post and the welfare of someone close to us.

Children also worry. Sometimes it is for trivial reasons and sometimes very serious. The most serious are often related to the welfare of close family or friends.

Children with special educational needs

A child has a special need when they are different from the rest of the class. All children are different, but these differences usually fall within a range we call 'normal'. A child with special needs falls outside this range and that special need will affect their ability to learn.

A special need is the underlying cause of an educational problem. I may, for example, say that Sam is three years behind in her reading. That in itself is not a special need. The special need may be that she is behind in her reading because she has a visual impairment or because she has dyslexia or because she has cerebral palsy. The special need is what comes after the word 'because' – this is what makes Sam different.

Sometimes a child becomes different for a short period of time, for a very special reason. Abdullah was different for about a month. He started to swear and became very aggressive to his classmates. It was his way of expressing his feelings when his mother died and he had to go and live with his aunt. For a month he was outside the boundaries of 'normal' for both his class and his school. His teacher kept a close eye on him and the headteacher kept in close contact with his

aunt. Together they helped Abdullah come to terms with his loss. He is now back in the range called normal. He doesn't have a special need any more.

Some children will always be different, for a very special reason. A car knocked down Tina when she was six. She broke an arm and a leg and suffered brain damage. Today, Tina walks with a limp, has no use of her left arm and finds it difficult to control her tongue and hence speak. She is likely to have these problems for the rest of her life. She has one-to-one support specifically to help her communicate and to help her move around school.

Schools have a system for categorising the level of help a child with special needs is given. It is based on a document called the SEN Code of Practice. There are four levels of support. These are listed in the table below.

A 'Statement' is not a certificate to prove that a child has a special need. It is, in fact, a contract. It is a contract between the principal carer, usually the parents, and the local authority. The contract states what additional resources the local authority will supply to a named school to enable the child's educational needs to be met at that school.

WHAT IT IS CALLED	WHAT IT MEANS
School Action	George has a problem. As teacher I tried a few things but got nowhere so I had a chat with the SEN coordinator, who suggested a few more things. We are trying those now.
School Action +	George has a problem. As teacher I tried a few things but got nowhere so I had a chat with the SEN coordinator, who suggested a few more. We tried those and still got nowhere so we went and found some help outside school. They suggested a few more things. We are trying those now. We have also started an Individual Education Plan (IEP) for George.
Assessment	George has a problem. As teacher I tried a few things but got nowhere so I had a chat with the SEN coordinator, who suggested a few more. We tried those and still got nowhere so we went and found some help outside school. We have also started an IEP for George. That suggested a few more things. We tried those and still got nowhere. Then someone suggested that we had an assessment to see if there were more specialist things we could do. We are in the process of the assessment now.
Statement	George has a problem. As teacher I tried a few things but got nowhere so I had a chat with the SEN coordinator, who suggested a few more. We tried those and still got nowhere so we went and found some help outside school. We have also started an IEP for George. That suggested a few more things. We tried those and still got nowhere. Then someone suggested that we had an assessment to see if there were more specialist things we can do. There were and, because the school couldn't provide them, George got a statement. Now he has a laptop and one-to-one support for 15 hours a week. (*Note:* George still has the problem.)

A statement is only required if additional resources are needed at the school. 'Additional' means anything over and above that already available in school.

Imagine I take George to school A and explain his needs to the headteacher. I then ask if the headteacher will take him. The headteacher says 'Yes! Of course!' No additional resources are needed and so I do not need a statement.

Now I take George to school B. I explain his needs to the headteacher. I then ask if the headteacher will take him. The headteacher says 'Yes! But...' Additional resources are needed, so a statement may be needed.

It really is that simple. Note that it is the headteacher who makes the decision. The process of assessment is finding out what the additional needs of the child are. Being told that you don't need a statement is simply saying that nothing extra is needed. It is not saying that the child does not have a special need.

So what are all these special needs? The table below lists the major educational groups. It is important to realise that a child with any of these will always have the condition. It can't be cured and there aren't any regular miracles. What is necessary is to give the child the tools they will need to deal with their problem during the rest of their life.

When the problem is acute, a statement is likely. The statement sets the direction the child needs to take. From this an IEP (Individual Education Plan) is produced, which shows which path is being travelled. From this a target is created that specifies the next step the child must take.

- *Direction*   Statement.
- *Path*   IEP.
- *Next step*   Target.

You will need to know the direction and the path. You may develop ideas and opinions in relation to each. However, your main task is to help the child take the next step. This requires patience, repetition, meticulous records, total consistency and a cheery disposition.

Suppose George has MLD. On Monday the class start on the 3 times table. On Tuesday they do it again. On Wednesday, the third repetition, nearly everyone has got it. On Thursday everyone is clued in, except George. The following week George does it every day and by the second Friday George has finally got it. But, by the following Monday, he has forgotten it again. That is what MLD is like. Continuous repetition is needed.

In this case you will need an endless supply of great ways to do the same thing again only differently. You are fortunate to have the Internet. Just go to www.google.com and type in "3 times table" (in double inverted commas). On 28 May 2004, it offered 681 links. These included 'the tables rap' (www.primaryresources.co.uk/english/tablesrap.htm),

TERMS USED FOR SPECIAL EDUCATIONAL NEEDS

MLD	Moderate learning difficulty (probably one key stage behind).
SLD	Severe learning difficulty (probably two key stages behind).
PMLD	Profound and multiple learning difficulties.
VI	Visual impairment.
HI	Hearing impairment.
ADHD/ADD	Attention deficit hyperactivity disorder.
PD	Physical disability, eg. cerebral palsy.
Speech & Language	eg. Cleft palate, speech impediment, language disorder.
SpLD	Specific learning difficulty – includes dyslexia and dyscalculia.
Emotion/Behaviour	Often combined as EBD – emotional and behavioural disorder.
Autism	Sometimes includes Asperger, Tourette and other syndromes.
Medical	Allergies, asthma, epilepsy, diabetes, etc.
G&T	Gifted and talented – children who excel at one or more things.

'Blast off with Drake'
(www.schools.ash.org.au/orps/blast_off.htm) and the 'Teacher Resource Exchange' (http://tre.ngfl.gov.uk). If you want an endless supply of great ideas, then look no further.

For George, you have to start sorting out what he will do and what he will miss. Clearly, when it takes George twice as long to do something, he is able to do only half as much. Sometimes you will need a statement to get the legal entitlement to modify and leave things out of the National Curriculum. At least the statement is more powerful than the National Curriculum. After all, the statement can modify the National Curriculum but the National Curriculum cannot modify the statement. That means George is more important than an arbitrary list of things to do and grades to achieve.

Following IEPs

You need to know the next step the child has to take. You also need to know which path you are on and where it will eventually take you. The IEP sets the general direction but you need a specific thing for a child to do. They are often badly worded and of little help. To make a difference you will have to make sense of the target first.

Some targets are negative. 'George has to stop hitting everyone who comes near him.' The problem with a negative target is you never know whether or not the intention was there. If Sarah walks past George without being thumped then George appears to have succeeded. However, we don't know that he chose not to hit her. He may have been occupied with something else, he may have been busy thumping Fred, he may even have been asleep!

Some targets are compound. 'George has to get his pen out and start working.' So which is the problem, the pen or the work? Someone has to make their mind up and then tell George.

Some targets are dependent. 'George must answer three questions every lesson.' This is an instruction to the teacher, not a target for George. If the teacher doesn't ask the questions then George can't succeed.

Some targets are learning objectives. 'George has to learn his number bonds to ten.' This is something that applies to all children. There is nothing special about it and it should not be a target. It is part of the National Curriculum. It is also a cop-out. Someone is failing to address the underlying problem and is settling for the symptoms instead.

Good targets are SMART – they are Simple,

Measurable, Achievable, Realistic and Timed. But that is not enough, you also have to know what success looks like. And so does George. How will George ever get it right if he doesn't know what 'right' is? OK, now you have a target and you know what success looks like. Now comes the crunch. This is the key message.

> **Top Tip**
> **Use every activity as an excuse to practise the target as often as possible.**

Keeping notes and records

Notes

About keeping notes – don't. If you must, then ask two simple questions. Firstly, the last set of notes you wrote – who read them? Secondly, why did they read them? You will need stunningly good answers to these questions if you are going to make notes.

There is an assistant in one school who carried a notebook around with her. She meticulously recorded everything. She had neat handwriting and wrote at length. She had been doing it for years. No one, including herself, had ever read them. Past volumes were kept at home, in case. In case of what? Whatever it was hadn't happened for years.

An alternative to notes? There is a classroom with 30 children, four of whom have a special need. On the wall is a small whiteboard for important notes. Any member of staff can record anything they have seen that is worthy of sharing. At the end of every day the team review what is on the board and decide if anything needs to be added to the single communal record kept on each child. This is excellent practice.

Records

About keeping records – absolutely essential. A good record has a few simple rules. It should

● be fast to complete

● focus on success/failure with one target

● contain no words other than the child's name, the target and a key to the way it is to be filled in

● tell you, at a glance, whether the child's performance against the target is improving.

If your records don't meet these simple tests then change your way of keeping records. You probably spend too much time writing copious notes about what happened and too little time thinking creatively about the fun you are going to create next. You are also in danger of complaining about the amount of time available rather than enthusing about working with children.

Attending review meetings

In preparation, gather together the targets the child has worked on and the records of how they got on.

When you arrive at the meeting you may find any or all of

- the headteacher and/or SEN coordinator, who will chair the meeting

- someone to take the minutes

- the key teacher(s) involved with the child

- the parents

- the child.

In addition, the school will have invited someone from the local authority to come. It's usually the educational psychologist who attends. There could then be a whole range of specialists, depending on the child's particular needs. For example, a physically disabled child may have a physiotherapist, an occupational therapist, a speech therapist and a nurse.

The annual review will (or should) follow a simple pattern. Firstly, there should be a review of the child's achievements since the last review. This is where you will be able to show what targets you have worked on and how well the child has performed against them. You may be asked questions about particular details. If you know then say so and, if you don't, then say you don't know.

There should then be a review of the next draft IEP. These are the paths to be followed in the next six months. Again, you may be asked for your ideas or opinions.

Finally, the meeting should decide whether the statement is still needed and, if it is, whether it is still worded correctly.

When your named child is absent

If you work one-to-one for four hours a day with a named child then you have to be available for four hours a day for that child.

But, note the wording – you have to be available. If the child is not in school, it does not affect your availability. You don't have to make it up some other time. It will make sense for you to do something else useful, as long as you are comfortable with what you are asked to do.

During any lesson, you have to be available. Your priority is to be available to your named child. That doesn't mean you have to hover over them and ignore everything else going on in the room.

A final thought

Good special needs support should make itself redundant. Education is about preparation for life. You won't be there in 20 years' time but the child will still have the special need. Your job is to teach them strategies for life without support. If you succeed then they won't need your support and you will be redundant. It is possible that this will be the first job you have ever done where you are out of work as soon as you succeed!

When working with children who have special needs, you have to slowly increase the distance between you and the child you support. At the start, you will have to hold their hand every step of the way. At the end, you will not even be required as a safety net. Success in dealing with special needs is keeping a clear vision of where the child is going and supporting them to get there themselves if at all possible.

Playground duties

Your role

Your key functions in the playground are

- dealing with accidents

- dealing with arguments

- promoting positive play.

Playground duty is not an arbitrary stroll round with a hot cup of tea. It should be carefully thought out and smoothly implemented. It all starts from your position. Your ability to be effective will depend on how many of you there are and where you each choose to stand.

There is a simple $n + 1$ rule for any playground. First you have to identify the smallest number of people needed to see every part of the playground. This is n, the minimum safe number. Now add 1 and this is the optimum number to manage the playground. The n people have static positions in the playground and have a particular direction to face. The $+1$ is free to roam or to rotate around the static positions, freeing up others who may otherwise get too cold.

The illustrations below show three playground layouts. Each shows the minimum number of assistants needed to see all parts of the playground (n). The arrows show the directions they should be facing to do this.

When you are on duty, you should have another adult in line of sight and you should be able to see the whole of your area. If your playground has trees or sheds in it, then you may need to be creative in finding the best place to stand. You may even have to place some areas out of bounds because you don't have enough staff to cover all the sight lines.

If you want to be sure you are right, then try the torch test. You will need a dark evening and a torch for each member of your team. Now stand in the places you think are critical. If you are right, then at least one of you should be able to shine your light on every bit of the playground surface without anyone moving. Now you know you've got it covered.

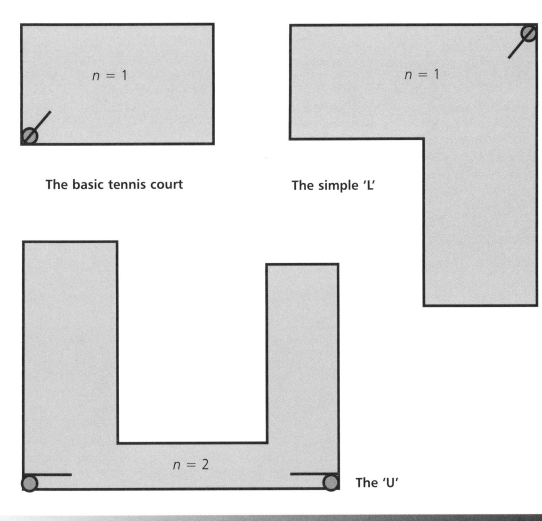

The basic tennis court

The simple 'L'

The 'U'

Now about that cup of tea – how would you feel if a child ran into you and they ended up covered in hot tea? How would you feel if you ended up covered in tea? If you'd feel good about either of these, take the tea out with you. If not, leave the tea inside while you do the playground duty.

You are in the playground with no tea standing where another member of your team can see you. Now what? There are two answers to this. Firstly, you need to consider your responsibilities. Children's safety is top of the list, followed by making sure they are all being nice to each other, and finally that they are 'playing nicely'. Secondly, you need to consider what you actually do. Top of the list is promoting positive play. You also want to make sure children are nice to each other, and finally you deal with any issues of health and safety.

These two lists are in reverse order. What you do is not in the same order of importance as what you are responsible for.

You will always be on the lookout for the things that go wrong but your principal concern is to promote positive play. That is what playground duty is all about.

Top Tip

Playground duty is about promoting positive play. Children choose playtime activities from their own experiences. These experiences are based on the television (football, cricket, etc.), video games (fighting and killing) and the latest crazes (the yo-yo – well, it's always in and out of fashion).

Children need to have a greater variety to choose from and they will only have that greater variety if someone teaches it to them. So, start teaching them new things to do at playtime. Don't make them too complicated or dependent on you. The children need to be able to play when you are not there. And don't make them stand around for long explanations. That is too much like the classroom and the children will get too cold waiting.

Playground duty is being a playleader and a cheerleader.

Dealing with accidents

The health and safety policy will tell you all you need to know about how to deal with accidents. There are laid-down procedures that need to be followed. Most playground injuries can be resolved with some kind words, a sticking plaster or some cold water. Occasionally you will be faced with a real medical emergency. You should already know about any children with allergies or medical conditions that need specific attention.

When someone is hurt, you have to decide the level of severity and then get help. If in any doubt, do not move the child unless leaving them where they are puts them in further danger. Moving an injured child could make matters worse. Similarly, if there is anything sticking into them, don't try taking it out.

You have to manage the situation. This means you have to secure the injured person and possibly manage the other children. If it is serious, you will need help. The previous section showed how this could be achieved as there should be another adult in your sight line, but, if you get really stuck, send children off in pairs to get help. Don't rely on sending one pair to one person. Be specific in your instructions to the children. 'I want you two to go together and tell Mrs Smith that there has been an accident and that I need help, now.' Now get them to tell you, 'What are you going to do?' Then confirm what they have to do. 'Well done, now go and find Mrs Smith and tell her I need help. Stay together.' You are now in with a chance that they will get it right. To improve the odds in your favour, send several pairs to different people. That way some of them might get through.

Expect to have to record what happened. Try to remember details – times, people and places are important. Try to write down what happened as soon as you can. You will certainly have to make a note in the school's accident record book. If you are not asked to do so, then make sure you ask for the book.

If you are left for any length of time, try to keep a record of events. Record anything that changes about the child and when it changed or started to change or when you happened to notice. Try to keep the child warm but not to the detriment of your own health. Don't give them anything to eat or drink – they may need an operation. Talk to them continuously, try to get their mind off their injury.

If you can, write everything down. It will help you to keep calm, it will prove valuable when completing the accident book and it may also prove invaluable to the medical team when they come to the child's aid.

Top Tip

Even the most minor accidents will need your attention and will mean you have to move. Work out the system for getting the attention of another member of your team in advance. One way is to send a message with a pair of children. You could use code words for the level of severity (as in all the emergency services).

Have a system of communication worked out in advance.

Dealing with arguments

Arguments come in all shapes and sizes. Boys tend to forget their disagreements and move on more quickly than girls, although boys' arguments can become explosive more quickly.

Your first objective should be early intervention. Experience will help you to spot an argument early on and then you can do something about it. Arguments tend to escalate because neither party will back down or because neither party is really listening to the other. Establishing a compromise or getting each to understand the other's point of view can quickly defuse the situation.

The key is discussion. Bring both parties to you and start talking. Make them take turns at talking and listening. Try not to judge the worth of what each says. Try instead to get them to follow the rules of discussion, ie. to take turns and to answer the points made. Above all, be seen to be fair and be seen to uphold the rules and values of the school. If the argument escalates it could end up in a pitched battle. The problems this creates for you are to

- deal with the combatants

- deal with the crowd.

Dealing with the combatants

This challenges one of the fundamental rules – never touch a child. However, help is at hand because your school should have a restraint policy (sometimes known as the 'physical restraint policy'). That policy will tell you some key things.

- *Physical restraint* is when you use force to protect or stop a child injuring himself or herself or someone else or seriously damaging property.

- *Injury* is a 'significant injury' to themselves or others, eg. bodily harm, abuse, life-threatening, etc.

- When you use physical restraint you must be certain that, if you hadn't, someone would have been injured.

In other words, if two children are fighting in the playground, you can get in there and stop them. What you can't do is wade in and knock them both out or tie them up and leave them there. You have to use the minimum force for the shortest possible time. The knock-out punch is quick but excessive – tying them up is slow and excessive.

The key ingredient is to keep talking, or at least to make a noise. One teacher splits up fights by singing 'You'll never walk alone!' while pushing in between the two who are fighting. It works for him. But then he is very large, very loud and tone deaf. Another teacher has a very large red ball which she pushes between the two having a fight. A third uses the expression 'What?' and 'Pardon?' repeatedly while squeezing in between. This has become so much part of that school's folklore that fights are measured by the combined count of 'whats?' and 'pardons?' Seventeen is considered severe.

In these examples, the point is that each person had a strategy. Each person kept calm, they didn't get angry or flustered. Each had a very clear purpose and having got between the combatants, each knew exactly what they were going to do next. All three had a strategy that relied on keeping the two apart. All three knew that their strategy would grab the attention of another member of staff. All three knew that the children had to have a cooling-off period before anything sensible would happen.

The key was that all three were confident because they had a strategy. We each have to find the right strategy for us. If you are of slight build, pregnant or infirm, then you may not have the confidence to wade in between two fighting children. You need to think what you would do long before you have to do it. Talk to others, preferably to those who have done it themselves. What did they do? What would they change next time? Now you can get your own strategy together.

> **Top Tip**
>
> Don't wait until a fight in the playground takes place before you work out how you will deal with it. Plan your strategy in advance. Now go over it in your mind until you have the confidence to do it.
>
> **Have a strategy for dealing with fights worked out in advance.**

Dealing with the crowd

The second problem is to deal with the crowd who are egging them on. Those who support the combatants must be made to realise that they are as much in the wrong as the two having the fight.

A headteacher, after separating two boys in the playground, took everyone into the school hall to debate the behaviour of the children who were egging them on. After about 20 minutes he was getting through. The children themselves were promoting tolerance and discussion. He started simply by asking everyone in the hall how they, as individuals, could have prevented the fight from starting. He went on to establish what signs the children should look for and, finally, how they could intervene in the future.

The head knew that, although he had yet to eliminate fights, he had reduced the number markedly and that those that still happened were shorter and much less vicious than previously. He also found that fights would be eliminated when the children realised that there were other ways to settle disputes.

Interestingly, throughout the whole fight and the follow-up, he didn't tell any child off at any point.

> **Top Tip**
>
> Use the aftermath of ugly incidents to encourage children to develop positive behaviour strategies. Get them to consider how they felt or would have felt.
>
> **Have a strategy for dealing with the crowd worked out in advance.**

Finally, remember that you are not alone. Make sure you have talked to someone in your school about what you would do in different situations. They may have some helpful suggestions to make.

Promoting positive play

Your first problem is the range of games that your children play. You have the opportunity to increase the range of games. Consider yourself as a play leader. Each day that you know you are on duty, advertise something like the following.

Game of the Week

DONGLEBATS

Everyone welcome

Explanation is at 10.45 in dustbin corner

Come alone or with friends

At 10.45 you make the two-minute explanation. You get one set of children to demonstrate. 'Any questions? Now you all have a go!'

Your second problem is to consider the children's attitude when they play their games. They need to feel positive about the activity and they need to enjoy themselves.

On the following pages, you will find a number of playground games that you can try. If you aren't up to the full-blown advert yet, try some games with a small and trusted group. You'll be surprised at the speed your small group grows.

Great games for the playground

Games for older children

Race and pace

You need at least four children.

Everyone puts one hand palm-down in the centre. The person whose first name is first in the alphabet goes first.

They touch the backs of the hands of each of the other children with their finger. Each time they touch a hand they say the word 'up'. Then, when no one is expecting it, they touch a hand and say 'away'.

Everyone rushes away as fast and as far as they can. The last person to be touched has to shout, 'Stop right now!'. As soon as they say 'now', everyone must stop.

Each person now takes shoe-length steps towards the person who said 'away'. The number of steps they take is the same as the number of letters in their first and last names added together.

The first person that can reach the one who shouted 'away' takes over as the one doing the touching. If no one can reach, then everyone starts again.

Hare and hound

You need lots of children in a circle. You also need a big ball and a small ball.

One person takes the small ball – this is the 'hare'. The person on the opposite side of the circle takes the big ball and this is the 'hound'. The balls get passed around the circle.

When a person holds either the hare or the hound they can pass in either direction and at any speed.

If you hold the hare, you must escape from the hound. If you hold the hound, you must catch the hare.

When the hare is passed, it goes from person to person.

When the hound is passed, it misses out the person next to you and goes to the one after them.

The game ends when one person is forced to hold the hare and the hound.

Tag

A game for any number of children.

One player is 'it'. The player who is 'it' has to chase the other players and touch one. The player who is touched then becomes 'it'.

A variation allows the player who is 'it' to name something that is 'home'. Any player touching the thing named as 'home' is safe. Only one player at a time can be safe. If another player arrives, the first has to leave.

Tag shadows

A further variation of Tag.

The game is identical to Tag, but now a player becomes 'it' when their shadow is touched.

Tail tag

A further variation on Tag.

The rules are the same as for Tag, only in this game every player has a 'tail'. The tail is a small piece of cloth, which may be tucked in a belt, passed through a buttonhole or poking out of a pocket.

All the players have a tail except the one who is 'it'. This player has to try to take a tail from someone else.

The person with no tail is always 'it' and has to try and get a tail.

The game can become more frantic when more than one person has no tail.

Squash

Up to four or five players with one wall and one ball.

Players take it in turns to strike the ball (either with their foot – 'football squash' – or with their hand – 'hand squash').

When struck, the ball must travel directly to the wall.

The player can hit the ball before it stops moving and can volley the ball.

A player is out when their shot fails to hit the wall before something else.

Tag bulldog

One person stands in the middle of the playground. Everyone else lines up on one side of the playground, touching the wall or fence. For safety reasons it is best to allocate one section of the playground for this game as anyone passing through as the players run could be hurt.

When the person in the middle shouts 'Go', everyone has to get to the opposite side of the playground and touch the wall or fence.

If the person in the middle touches them before they touch the other side, then they are tagged.

A tagged person joins the person in the middle.

Eventually, everyone will be in the middle trying to catch the last person. When they do, the last person becomes the first in the middle for the next round.

Ball tag bulldog

A variation on Tag bulldog.

The game is played the same way as Tag bulldog. In this game the children in the middle each have a ball. They tag the runners by hitting them on the legs with the ball. The ball must be thrown and not kicked.

Mad Mitch

One child is Mad Mitch. All the rest have to do a silly walk. They have to move around using their silly walk only. Each silly walk must be a single repeated pattern.

Whenever she or he is ready, Mad Mitch starts to copy a silly walk. As soon as a silly walk is copied, that person has to stand still. If they don't, they are out.

As soon as Mad Mitch stops doing their silly walk, they must start again. Failure to start when Mad Mitch stops means that they are out.

As soon as one person is out, they become the judge as to whether any other person is out or not.

Each person who is out makes the panel of judges bigger.

French cricket

One person stands still and has a tennis racquet or a cricket bat.

The rest of the players have to try and hit the player on the legs with a tennis ball.

The player with the racquet/bat can protect him or herself and hit the ball away.

Players throwing the ball must throw from where they first touched the ball.

Players can pass the ball any number of times before throwing but can only change position in an attempt to retrieve the ball from the racquet/bat.

The player who successfully strikes the legs is the next to hold the racquet/bat.

Touching letters

The person whose first name is first in the alphabet goes first.

They shout a letter of the alphabet, any letter. Everyone must now touch something – anything – which starts with that letter.

As soon as everyone has touched, the first person to touch something with that letter calls the next letter, which must be different.

Only one person can touch any one object. The more people that play, the more difficult it gets.

Last laugh

One child is the comedian. The rest of the group are the audience.

The audience can stand anywhere and face any direction. They must then stand still.

The comedian has to make the audience laugh. The comedian can move around but may not shout or touch any member of the audience.

Any member of the audience who laughs is out, and joins the comedian trying to make the rest laugh.

The last person to laugh is the new comedian and the game starts all over again.

Fall about

One person is the caller. The rest are in twos or threes.

The caller shouts out a number of feet and a number of hands.

Each team of two or three now has to create a balance with only the named number of hands and feet in touch with the ground.

If a team falls over, then one of that team must swap with the caller.

The caller can change the number of hands and feet as quickly or as slowly as they wish. The longer the pause, the more difficult it will be to hold some balance positions.

The caller may not change the call until at least one team has managed the balance with the last call.

Marching time

One person is the sergeant major and the rest are the troops.

The sergeant major lines the troops up so that they are in one line, arm's length apart.

The sergeant major now gives instructions, for example, 'Forward march', 'Left turn', 'About turn', etc.

The sergeant major is trying to make someone go wrong.

The first person to go wrong becomes the new sergeant major and starts all over again.

If the sergeant major gives the troops an impossible instruction or marches them into a brick wall, then the sergeant major has to take them all back to the start and begin again.

Games for younger children

Younger children will enjoy some of the traditional games such as Ring-a-ring-o-roses, The farmer's in his den, There was a princess long ago. These and other ring games may be taught in class or you can find books full of ideas for variations on these themes in the library.

Peek-a-boo

Any number of players.

One player stands with their back to the others. The rest start behind a line some 10 metres or more away.

Whenever the player at the front has their back turned, the rest can move forward.

The player at the front can turn round at any time. When they do, if they see someone moving, that person is sent back to the start.

The object is to be the first player to touch the person at the front without being seen moving. This person then takes over as the player at the front.

Please, Mr Crocodile

Any number of players.

One child is Mr Crocodile and stands at the front.

The others stand in a line about 10 metres away, and call out 'Please Mr Crocodile, may we cross your golden river to reach the other side?' He replies 'Only if you have a (names a letter) in your name.'

Mr Crocodile turns his back while the children step the appropriate number of paces forward for the number of times that letter appears in their name. As soon as someone reaches Mr Crocodile, they touch him and he chases them all. The one who is caught takes the part of Mr Crocodile the next time.

Hide and seek

Any number of players.

One child closes their eyes and counts to 20. Everyone else goes to hide.

When the child who is counting reaches 20, they go in search of the others. Each time they find someone, the extra person also has to find the others.

The last person found is the next to start counting.

Time-fillers ('Plan B')

'Plan B' is what you do when 'Plan A' doesn't work. Plan A was having a teacher around. Plan A was an activity that was supposed to last 20 minutes. Plan B is for when the teacher has gone missing or the activity lasts just five minutes. Plan B is what you do when, having collected the class from the playground, you take them to the classroom and find no teacher waiting.

Plan B was what one assistant did in the rain outside the swimming pool with 14 Year 5 children because the minibus broke down. Plan B is what the assistant in Reception did when the sand in the the sand pit needed changing. Plan B is what the assistant did for the five minutes before home time because the teacher had been called out to see a parent.

What makes a good Plan B?

A good Plan B is something you can do with any number of children, of any age and of any range of ability. It can be done anywhere, any time and with no resources. It can last as long as you like but, when you stop, it is finished.

You should always have at least two Plan Bs up your sleeve just in case. You should want to use them so much that instead of dreading being left with a load of kids, you are actually looking forward to it. You should be looking forward to getting the children involved.

There are a few ideas on the following pages. Every idea has been seen in use, brilliantly, in a real school with real children. In each case the assistant led the children into the activity with confidence. Where did the confidence come from? It came from having practised the ideas first. Try each one you want to use on real people first. Then you can get to see how best to lead it. Well, that's your next dinner party sorted!

In every case, the secret ingredient was there in abundance. What is the secret ingredient? It's having FUN! The children will love these games. Yes, they are games. Children learn a lot through games and one really good teaching strategy is to use games to introduce, practise and reinforce. That is exactly what these Plan Bs will do.

Children will become totally absorbed in them. One of these was used by an assistant at the end of an assembly. It enabled her to get the whole of Year 6 from the hall to the classroom, sitting down and working, in total silence without the assistant saying a single word. The children had something to think about and just wanted to get back to their books so that they could write it down.

The examples here are all based in either numeracy or literacy. No teacher will ever stop you using them since they encourage children to practise and develop their skills with language and number.

This is also a problem for you. The teachers are going to see how good these games are and then they will use them as well. So keep one or two up your sleeve for when they do.

Be on the look-out for more great ideas. They crop up all the time. One occurred in a geography lesson where one group were trying to find a city for every letter of the alphabet while another group were taking it in turns to name a city, not named before, that started with the last letter of the previous contribution. Sounds easy, until you try it. But then that's what Plan B is all about – trying it.

The answer is 42

Tell the children that the answer is 42. Now ask them what the question was. Start by telling them that the question includes a +, then try a −. You can move on to multiple signs or even times and divide. With younger children make the target number between 1 and 10.

Older or more able children can be given a much harder target. Try 20 per cent, 2.5, or 'a multiple of six'. If you get fed up with your first target, try another target. If you start losing eye contact, it is too difficult.

Give me a number

Get individuals to give you a number. You then perform an operation on the number and give them the answer. They have to work out what operation you are doing.

Single operations (+1, +3, x4, etc.) are quite easy. Double operations (+3x2) are more difficult and can usually be expressed in two ways (+3x2 = x2+6). Triple operations are very difficult (+2x4−1) and should be used sparingly.

Children may need to keep a record of their answers to help them spot the pattern. You can go for other rules like 'next highest number that is prime', 'next multiple of four', etc.

With these four numbers

Give children four single-digit numbers and a target. They can use any or all of the numbers and any operations to make the target. Then add one to the target and carry on.

You should be able to make any number between 1 and 100 given any four different single-digit numbers. For example, given 3, 5, 7, 8,

$$50 = (3 + 7) \times 5$$
$$51 = 7 \times 8 - 5$$
$$52 = (7 - 3) \times (8 + 5)$$
$$53 = 7 \times 8 - 3$$
$$54 = 7 \times 8 - 5 + 3$$

Another idea for younger children

Sing number rhymes and songs with younger children. Be on the lookout for new ones to teach them.

Stand up, sit down

One child asks the questions and each of the other children thinks of a number. The questioner now poses a series of questions, such as 'are you odd?', 'are you less than 50?', etc.

Each time a question is asked, children whose number means they can answer 'Yes' stand up. If their answer is 'No' they sit down.

The challenge is for the person asking the questions to get everyone to stand up. You make it more difficult if you do not allow children to use 'greater than' or 'less than' in their questions.

Legs!

Children work in groups of four or five (less for younger children). Each child thinks of something with legs (a spider, a football team, a horse and rider, etc.).

They now have to use each of the things with legs to make a sum. (For example, the king and queen and two chairs is equal to a spider, a man and a robin).

Personal numbers

Split the children into groups. Younger children need smaller groups. Each child picks any number between 0 and 9. They line up to make a number. (Suppose the children picked 5, 7 and 4. They could line up as 574.)

The teacher now calls out types of number and they have to change places to make it. (For example, make an even number – 574, a different even number – 754, an odd number – 475, etc.).

Two people, one half

A game played in pairs. One child thinks of a number related to something (eg. 22 is the number of legs on a football team).

The other child thinks of something that is associated with half the number (11 is the number of players in a hockey team). They now think of another number associated with this (eg. 1 goalkeeper) and give half of that number (eg. 1/2).

They continue to take turns in this way.

Found poetry

Get someone to give you a subject. Everyone now thinks of a word to go with the subject. It doesn't matter if children pick the same word. They now say the words in turn to make a poem whose title is the original subject.

With older children you can ask them to put their word in a sentence. More able children can then be asked to reduce their sentence to three or four words that retain the meaning. Each time these are repeated in turn.

Children can have a lot of fun by changing places and so reordering the lines in their poem. Given enough children, you can group them into verses. You could start by insisting the initial letter sound of the first word was common or that the original words should all end in 'y' and be at the end of their sentences.

The never-ending story 1

Give children a starting location (eg. 'You are standing in a dark, dank wood next to a small, slowly flowing stream…') then introduce a character ('you suddenly realise that, sitting by the stream under the leaf of a stinging nettle, is a large brown toad…'). Now add a touch of the impossible ('who turns to you, winks, and remarks that "Tuesday is such a surprising day!"'). Finally, you throw in the challenge ('you are alarmed, not because the toad can talk, or even that it's Tuesday and the toad is surprised, but because…'). In pairs or small groups the children have to finish the story and then recount their ending to everybody else. If more time is available, you add a final line which they then must carry on from ('and then you woke up and found…').

The never-ending story 2

Give children a theme (food, for example). They now have to build a story about the theme using one word each. The first child has to start the story and the last has to finish it.

When the one-word-each story is done, the group has to add a second word each. The story must still have a beginning, middle and an end. Children can add punctuation as they progress. When the two-word-each story is done, they each add a third word, and so on.

The number plate game

Give children the three letters from a number plate and a subject (eg. RNK, food) they have to think of three words starting with the letters R, N and K which make sense when put together and are about the subject (eg. 'Really Nice Kebabs'). Whoever gives the answer picks the next subject (eg. shopping – 'Rachel Needs Kickers') and you keep going until you run out of subjects. Then you change the letters.

With young children, get them to say the words that have each letter as an initial sound. Older children have to find a single word that has all three letters in it in that order. They then tell you how many letters they have (eg. 'roughnecks' has 10 letters).

Nursery mimes

In groups the children have to pick a nursery rhyme and then act it out so that the rest can guess which it is.

Finish, don't finish

The children all start with three lives. The first person thinks of a word and gives everyone the first letter (eg. P). The second person thinks of a word starting with P and gives the second (eg. E). The third person has to think of a word starting with PE and add the third letter. At no point can a person finish a word. (I may have been thinking of PETROL so I add a T, but this makes PET which is a word.) If a person does make a word, they lose a life and start the next round. If someone adds a letter and you don't think it makes a word, you challenge them. If you are right then they lose a life but if it really was a word, you lose the life.

Letter words

Each child picks a letter. They now have to make as many words as they can with the letters in two minutes. They score one point for each letter in each word. Bigger groups give more letters and make it easier. Older children can get into groups as small as five and you can get them to give you adjectives only.

Routine tasks

Routine tasks are those little jobs that need doing and which take time. Among them could be any or all of the following. In each case there are a few suggestions of things you could check whenever you have some spare moments.

For the next session

- Are the resources all out and ready?
- Is there any photocopying that needs doing?

The class library

- Are all the books in the correct places?
- Are there any books in need of repair?
- Are there any books that need to be returned to a central location?

The school library

- Are there returned books that need putting back on the shelves?
- Are there new books that need to be stamped, covered or catalogued?
- Are there books that are in the wrong places?
- Are there any books that need to be repaired?
- Is the display in need of changing or repairing?
- Is the room tidy?

The home–school bags

- Are there any letters that need to be put in the school bags to go home?
- Are the readers in the bags ready to go home?
- Has any money or a note been left in a home–school bag?

The tables

- Are the children's tables all tidy?
- Are the resources on each table complete?
- Do any pencils need sharpening?
- Have any children left things out that should be in their trays?

The classroom store cupboard

- Does it need tidying?
- Is there anything missing or running low that can be replenished?

The stock room

- Does it need tidying?
- Is there anything missing or running low that can be replenished?

Lost property

- Does it need tidying?
- Are there new items to be added?
- Are there any items that are due to be thrown away?

The art materials

- Are the palettes clean and dry?
- Are the brushes washed and dry and the right way up?
- Do the resources need sorting or tidying?
- Are there sufficient quantities of paint and paper?
- Do the drying racks need emptying?

The computers

- Are they switched on and working?
- Does the printer actually print?
- Does the printer need more paper or ink?
- Does the network link work?
- Has each mouse still got its ball and mat?
- Are the screens clean?

The classroom display

- Is there anything that needs to be repaired or re-fixed?
- Is there a section that needs to be taken down or put up?
- Does any work need framing or mounting?
- Are there any titles or labels to be made?

Generally

- Is there any clearing up needing to be done in the classroom?
- Are there any mugs or cups that need to go back to the staffroom?
- Do the class pets need food, water or a good spring clean?
- Do the plants need watering?

Finally

- Have all the pigs been fed, watered and made ready to fly?